Frogstomp

33 1/3 Global

33 1/3 Global, a series related to but independent from **33 1/3**, takes the format of the original series of short, music-based books and brings the focus to music throughout the world. With initial volumes focusing on Japanese and Brazilian music, the series will also include volumes on the popular music of Australia/Oceania, Europe, Africa, the Middle East, and more.

33 1/3 Japan

Series Editor: Noriko Manabe

Spanning a range of artists and genres – from the 1970s rock of Happy End to technopop band Yellow Magic Orchestra, the Shibuya-kei of Cornelius, classic anime series *Cowboy Bebop*, J-Pop/EDM hybrid Perfume, and vocaloid star Hatsune Miku – **33 1/3 Japan** is a series devoted to in-depth examination of Japanese popular music of the twentieth and twenty-first centuries.

Published Titles:

Supercell's *Supercell* by Keisuke Yamada

AKB48 by Patrick W. Galbraith and Jason G. Karlin

Yoko Kanno's *Cowboy Bebop Soundtrack* by Rose Bridges

Perfume's *Game* by Patrick St. Michel

Cornelius's *Fantasma* by Martin Roberts

Joe Hisaishi's *My Neighbor Totoro: Soundtrack* by Kunio Hara

Shonen Knife's *Happy Hour* by Brooke McCorkle

Nenes' *Koza Dabasa* by Henry Johnson

Yuming's *The 14th Moon* by Lasse Lehtonen

Toshiko Akiyoshi-Lew Tabackin Big Band's *Kogun* by E. Taylor Atkins

S.O.B.'s *Don't Be Swindle* by Mahon Murphy and Ran Zwigenberg

Forthcoming Titles:

Kohaku Utagassen: The Red and White Song Contest by Shelley Brunt

Yellow Magic Orchestra's *Yellow Magic Orchestra* by Toshiyuki Ohwada

Modeselektor's *Happy Birthday!* by Sean Nye

Mercyful Fate's *Don't Break the Oath* by Henrik Marstal

Bea Playa's *I'll Be Your Plaything* by Anna Szemere and András Rónai

Various Artists' *DJs do Guetto* by Richard Elliott

Czesław Niemen's *Niemen Enigmatic* by Ewa Mazierska and Mariusz Gradowski

Massada's *Astaganaga* by Lutgard Mutsaers

Los Rodriguez's *Sin Documentos* by Fernán del Val and Héctor Fouce

Édith Piaf's *Récital 1961* by David Looseley

Nuovo Canzoniere Italiano's *Bella Ciao* by Jacopo Tomatis

Iannis Xenakis's *Persepolis* by Aram Yardumian

Vopli Vidopliassova's *Tantsi* by Maria Sonevytsky

Amália Rodrigues's *Amália at the Olympia* by Lila Ellen Gray

Ardit Gjebrea's *Projekt Jon* by Nicholas Tochka

Aqua's *Aquarium* by C. C. McKee

J.M.K.E.'s *To the Cold Land* by Brigitta Davidjants

Taco Hemingway's *Jarmark* by Kamila Rymajdo

Einstürzende Neubauten's *Kollaps* by Melle Jan Kromhout and Jan Nieuwenhuis

Forthcoming Titles:

Tripes' *Kefali Gemato Hrisafi* by Dafni Tragaki

Silly's *Februar* by Michael Rauhut

CCCP's *Fedeli Alla Linea's 1964-1985 Affinità-Divergenze Fra Il Compagno Togliatti E Noi Del Conseguimento Della Maggiore Età* by Giacomo Bottà

Sigur Rós' *Ágætis Byrjun* by Tore Størvold

33 1/3 Oceania

Series Editors: Jon Stratton (senior editor) and Jon Dale (specializing in books on albums from Aotearoa/New Zealand)

Spanning a range of artists and genres from Australian Indigenous artists to Maori and Pasifika artists, from Aotearoa/New Zealand noise music to Australian rock, and including music from Papua and other

Pacific islands, **33 1/3 Oceania** offers exciting accounts of albums that illustrate the wide range of music made in the Oceania region.

Published Titles:
John Farnham's *Whispering Jack* by Graeme Turner
The Church's *Starfish* by Chris Gibson
Regurgitator's *Unit* by Lachlan Goold and Lauren Istvandity
Kylie Minogue's *Kylie* by Adrian Renzo and Liz Giuffre
Alastair Riddell's *Space Waltz* by Ian Chapman
Hunters & Collectorss *Human Frailty* by Jon Stratton
The Front Lawn's *Songs from the Front Lawn* by Matthew Bannister
Bic Runga's *Drive* by Henry Johnson
The Dead C's *Clyma est mort* by Darren Jorgensen
Ed Kuepper's *Honey Steel's Gold* by John Encarnacao
Chain's *Toward the Blues* by Peter Beilharz
Hilltop Hoods' *The Calling* by Dianne Rodger
Screamfeeder's *Kitten Licks* by Ben Green and Ian Rogers
The Clean's *Boodle Boodle Boodle* by Geoff Stahl
The Avalanches' *Since I Left You* by Charles Fairchild
John Sangster's *Lord of the Rings Vols. 1–3* by Bruce Johnson
Soundtrack from *Saturday Night Fever* by Clinton Walker
Eyeliner's *BUY NOW* by Michael Brown
TISM's *Machiavelli and the Four Seasons* by Tyler Jenke
Crowded House's *Together Alone* by Barnaby Smith
silverchair's *Frogstomp* by Jay Daniel Thompson

Forthcoming Titles:
The Triffids' *Born Sandy Devotional* by Christina Ballico
5MMM's *Compilation Album of Adelaide Bands 1980* by Collette Snowden
INXS' *Kick* by Lauren Moxey
Sunnyboys *Sunnyboys* by Stephen Bruel
The La De Das' *The Happy Prince* by John Tebbutt

Gary Shearston's *Dingo* by Peter Mills
Kate Ceberano's *Brave* by Panizza Allmark
Robert Forster's *Danger in the Past* by Patrick Chapman
Various Artists' *A Truckload of Sky: The Lost Songs of David McComb* by
    Glenn D'Cruz
Dinah Lee's *Introducing Dinah Lee* by Kimberly Cannady
The Waifs' *Up All Night* by Rebecca Bennison
The Three Out's *Move* by James Gaunt
Split Enz' *Mental Notes* by Michael Lamb
Tame Impala's *Currents* by Alister Newstead

33 1/3 South Asia

Series Editor: Natalie Sarrazin

From the films of Bollywood and Lollywood, to home-grown *bhangra* hip-hop, Hindu devotional pop and Sufi rock, Sri Lankan rap, Indo jazz and disco, new-wave electronica and diasporic Asian Underground scene, **33 1/3 South Asia** takes readers on a sonically diverse journey through the most significant soundtracks and albums from the twentieth and twenty-first centuries.

Published:

Dil Chahta Hai Soundtrack by Jayson Beaster-Jones
Lata Mangeshkar's *My Favourites, Volume 2* by Anirudha Bhattacharjee
    and Chandrashekhar Rao
Coke Studio (Season 14) by Rakae Rehman Jamil and Khadija Muzaffar

33 1/3 Africa

Series Editor: Michael Veal

33 1/3 Africa is a series of books on canonical, album-length works of African music including traditional music, experimental music, and, with particular emphasis, popular music. Academic and journalistic writing results in sophisticated, nuanced and accessible narratives on African music.

Published:

Fela Anikulapo-Kuti's *Sorrow Tears and Blood* by Stephanie Shonekan

Forthcoming Titles:

Cesária Évora's *Miss Perfumado* by Jacqueline Georgis

Paul Simon's *Graceland* by Kalvin Schmidt-Rimpler Dinh

Nico, Rochereau, Roger & L'African Fiesta – *Volume 1 (1962-1963)* by
    Frank Gunderson

Frogstomp

Jay Daniel Thompson

Series Editors: Jon Stratton, UniSA Creative, University of South Australia, and Jon Dale, University of Melbourne, Australia

BLOOMSBURY ACADEMIC

NEW YORK • LONDON • OXFORD • NEW DELHI • SYDNEY

BLOOMSBURY ACADEMIC
Bloomsbury Publishing Inc, 1385 Broadway, New York, NY 10018, USA
Bloomsbury Publishing Plc, 50 Bedford Square, London, WC1B 3DP, UK
Bloomsbury Publishing Ireland, 29 Earlsfort Terrace, Dublin 2, D02 AY28, Ireland

BLOOMSBURY, BLOOMSBURY ACADEMIC and the Diana logo are trademarks of
Bloomsbury Publishing Plc

First published in the United States of America 2025

Library of Congress Cataloging-in-Publication Data
Names: Thompson, Jay Daniel, author.
Title: Frogstomp / Jay Daniel Thompson.
Description: New York : Bloomsbury Academic, 2025. | Series: 33 1/3 Oceania
| Includes bibliographical references and index. | Summary: "Australian
rock band Silverchair released Frogstomp in 1995, and it became a global
sensation. Its success has often been attributed to an imitation of
North American grunge bands and its capitalization of Gen X angst. This
book argues that Frogstomp is culturally significant on its own terms
due to its reflection of the impact of globalization on Australian music
in the late 20th century and because of its eclectic, and little
discussed, array of pop culture influences. Engaging with Australian
1990s popular culture and grunge music and analyzing Silverchair's
performance at the MTV and ARIA Music Awards in 1995, Frogstomp is seen
here in a distinctive new light"– Provided by publisher.
Identifiers: LCCN 2024056321 (print) | LCCN 2024056322 (ebook) | ISBN
9798765113349 (paperback) | ISBN 9798765113332 (hardback) | ISBN
9798765113356 (epub) | ISBN 9798765113363 (ebook)
Subjects: LCSH: Silverchair (Musical group). Frogstomp. | Rock
music–Australia–1991-2000–History and criticism. | Grunge
music–Australia–History and criticism.
Classification: LCC ML421.S525 T46 2025 (print) | LCC ML421.S525 (ebook)
| DDC 782.42166092/2–dc23/eng/20241213
LC record available at https://lccn.loc.gov/2024056321
LC ebook record available at https://lccn.loc.gov/2024056322

ISBN: HB: 979-8-7651-1333-2
       PB: 979-8-7651-1334-9
    ePDF: 979-8-7651-1336-3
   eBook: 979-8-7651-1335-6

Series: 33 1/3 Oceania

Typeset by Deanta Global Publishing Services, Chennai, India
Printed and bound in the United States of America

For product safety related questions contact productsafety@bloomsbury.com.

To find out more about our authors and books visit www.bloomsbury.com and sign
up for our newsletters.

For the 1990s teenagers everywhere

Contents

Acknowledgements

I thank Jon Stratton, Jon Dale and the team at Bloomsbury for commissioning this manuscript and providing the opportunity to revisit the 1990s.

I thank my colleagues in the School of Media and Communication at RMIT University, especially Catherine Strong for her important scholarship on grunge music, Lisa Waller and Diana Bossio for their support, Eddy Hurcombe and Sam Whiting for being brilliant officemates, and the professional staff (especially Tania Vitale, Karli Lukas, Anastasia Bezsmertna and Rachael Alexander) for their tireless work. Big ups to the following folk for providing useful references: Hugh Davies, Alex Griffin, Jim McCormack and Rosie Overell. Catherine Gomes has always been an excellent role model with her work ethic and good humour.

I owe a huge debt of gratitude to my family and friends, who are too numerous to name here. Catharine Lumby deserves a special mention for believing in me as a researcher and for our amusing chats about pop culture and Newcastle. My parents, Trish and Peter, deserve praise for enduring the grunge music blaring from my bedroom during my teenage years. My cat, Charlie, reminds me to take breaks from typing.

Thanks to the friend who allowed me to record his copy of *Frogstomp* onto cassette all those summers ago.

Finally, kudos to silverchair themselves for providing the soundtrack to a glorious era.

Author's Note

The band's name will be spelled using a lower-case 's', as this was the spelling during the *Frogstomp* era. silverchair would start to use the capital 'S' around the time their *Diorama* album was released in 2002 (SMH 2002). Throughout the book, the capital 'S' is used only when quoting secondary sources and when describing the band's activities during and after the *Diorama* period.

Introduction

'Wait till tomorrow!'

Those lyrics growled out of CD players and car radios everywhere in 1995. 'Tomorrow' was the breakout single for Newcastle rock trio silverchair and appeared on their debut album *Frogstomp*, which propelled the group to international stardom. This was no mean feat for a group of teenagers, though of course that youthfulness was a major selling point and an inspiration for other pubescent musos. Those musos were energized by the overnight success of those likely lads who had emerged seemingly from nowhere. They include Ella Hooper, who founded the band Killing Heidi with her brother Jesse in 1996. Hooper recalls Jesse saying: 'Look! They're three young dudes from Newcastle. We're two young kids from the country. If they can do it, we can' (cited in Stapleton 2014).

The band – comprising singer Daniel Johns, drummer Ben Gillies and bassist Chris Joannou – began in 1992 as Innocent Criminals, playing out of garages in the traditionally working-class, surfing-oriented Newcastle. Their big break came in June 1994, when the group won a competition run by the Special Broadcasting Service (SBS) TV show *Nomad* and radio station triple j. The competition was won on the strength of 'Tomorrow', which shot to number one on the Australian Recording Industry Association (ARIA) charts later that year and stayed there for six weeks (Stapleton 2014). *Frogstomp* was released in March 1995 and became a huge hit, reaching the number one spot on music charts in Australia and New Zealand and number nine on America's Billboard 200, and selling three million copies globally (Hedger 2020; Jolly 2018).

This book argues that *Frogstomp* marks a profoundly significant moment in the history of Australian music. To truly appreciate this significance, it's necessary to acknowledge but also move beyond the three dominant ways in which this popularity has been framed. On their own, these framings do not enable a nuanced perspective on the album's inception and prosperity.

The first frame can be described as 'Nirvana in pyjamas', after a jingle that referenced the Australian children's TV program *Bananas in Pyjamas* and that would haunt the band during their formative years. This frame is premised on the view that *Frogstomp*-era silverchair was a cheap, childish imitation of North American grunge acts. Johns' vocals resembled those of Pearl Jam's Eddie Vedder, and he physically resembled Nirvana's Kurt Cobain – observations made by none other than Cobain's widow, Courtney Love, frontwoman of Hole (Apter 2018: 36). The distorted guitars and anguished vocals could have been lifted from any of the Seattle acts who were charting on 'alternative' radio. The band's youth was frequently mentioned in interviews; for instance, a piece in the music magazine *Juice* mentions that the members were accompanied on tour by their parents (Mathieson 1999: 128). In October 1995, the Australian comedy act Silverpram released a parody of 'Tomorrow', in which their protagonist celebrated turning the grand old age of four.

The second frame, and one which is intimately related to the first, holds that grunge bands such as silverchair expressed the angst and ennui endured by members of the so-called Generation X. This was the media moniker assigned to folk born between the early 1960s and early 1980s. silverchair members were all born in 1979, and their music was replete with lyrics about hatred, suffering and execution.

The third frame can be described as 'local boys made good'. The band began playing out of garages in Newcastle, a seaside city located 150 kilometres north of Sydney, in the Hunter Region of northern New South Wales, in what was known as Mulubinba by the traditional Aboriginal custodians (McGurk and Rowe 2001: 55). Newcastle is well known for its sporting cultures, most notably surfing and rugby league. The city has also been a key site of Australian manufacturing, including coal mining, shipbuilding, textiles and steelmaking – the latter of which has been described as 'the industry around which Newcastle's identity in the Australian cultural system of space has been constructed' (McGuirk and Rowe 2001: 55).

The city's manufacturing sector took a substantial hit during the early 1990s recession, as one writer points out:

Just as Newcastle stood for Australia's shining future during the 'resources boom' of the early 1980s, it has been a major symbol by which Australians have understood the decline of manufacturing in the later deregulated economy. The retrenchments at the BHP steelworks, the closure of the state dockyards, the failure to win the shipbuilding contract for the new navy frigates ... (Metcalfe 1993: 1)

To the best of my knowledge, the silverchair members have not described being directly impacted by the job losses described above, for example, with family members being made unemployed. The recession and its impact on Newcastle industries did provide the backdrop for the writing and production of *Frogstomp* and may well have indirectly influenced the contents, which, as Chapter 2 explains, are indeed bleak.

Importantly, Newcastle is not renowned as a musical destination; indeed, within the wider Australian music industry, the city has sometimes been marginalized. A 2020 study points out that 'the nation's local music scenes remain concentrated in urban areas, particularly the larger east coast cities of Brisbane, Sydney, and Melbourne' (Rogers and Whiting 2020: 452). Even Australian bands on tour can bypass regional cities such as Newcastle due to cost and a lack of interest from booking agencies. A 1998 report noted that the major Australian recording studios were then based in Melbourne and Sydney, and thus regional musicians had to travel great distances to use these facilities and to build their careers (Groeneveld 1998: 28; cited in McIntyre and Sheather 2013: 44).

Those frames certainly have their truths. *Frogstomp*-era silverchair *were* teenagers whose sound *did* resemble that of Pearl Jam. The silverchair of 1995 *did* express anti-commercial sentiments not unlike those aired by Nirvana. They *did* produce some bleak tunes and would continue to do so as the years passed – 'Cemetery' (from 1997's *Freak Show*) and 'Ana's Song' (from 1999's *Neon Ballroom*) are two post-grunge examples. silverchair did take shape in a location that was better known for its light industry than its music scene (though, as Chapter 1 describes, that scene has indeed been lively).

Yet, the frames are limited insofar as they gloss over the plethora of cultural references evident throughout *Frogstomp* and the specificities of the sociohistorical milieu in which the album was produced. This was a milieu shaped thoroughly by globalization, neoliberalism and economic recession. The frames also gloss over the album's remarkable and under-remarked tonal shift, from despair to an optimism that's not usually associated with grunge.

This book will explore those factors in greater detail and, in doing so, explicate *Frogstomp*'s cultural significance.

Chapter 1 situates *Frogstomp*'s production within what Arjun Appadurai (1996) terms 'global cultural flows'. This framework helps explain how trends and fashions are distributed across countries and cultures, and, in doing so, they are shaped by the particularities of those countries and cultures. *Frogstomp* may be influenced by Seattle sounds, but its production is also the result of specifically Australian actors, musical genres and studios. The latter includes radio station triple j, which was run by the national broadcaster, Australian Broadcasting Commission (ABC), and which was carving out a niche as a station that catered to a youthful audience and showcased 'alternative' Australian music. This chapter also situates silverchair's debut album within the context of economic transformations and upheavals that were unfolding globally during the 1980s and 1990s. These include both neoliberalism and a global recession that impacted on young people particularly badly. I suggest that this impact has helped shape the Generation X (hereafter 'GenX') stereotype and the supposed stand-off between this generation and the Baby Boomers. These generational stereotypes are simplistic, as is the reading of grunge as an outlet for GenX angst, but it's worth acknowledging that both have some basis in reality.

Chapter 2 opens with an overview of *Frogstomp*'s production. This section especially emphasizes the important role played by the producer, Kevin 'Caveman' Shirley. The chapter proceeds to analyse each album track, in doing so highlighting their myriad cultural references, as well as the album's distinct tonal shift from darkness to light. There is discussion about the band's promotional campaign, chart success and interactions with fans. Chapter 2 concludes by examining a selection of *Frogstomp* reviews published in the Australian and North American music and mainstream press. Those responses (which ranged from effusive to dismissive) echoed and contributed to the above-mentioned framings of silverchair and their album.

Chapter 3 focuses on silverchair as a live act. Specifically, this chapter studies three live performances: the recording of 'Pure Massacre' at Sydney's Phoenician Club in December 1994 that formed the basis of that song's Australian music video; their Big Day Out festival performances in January–February 1995; and their cheeky (non-)appearances at the ARIA Awards ceremony in October 1995. All three case studies demonstrate how silverchair constructed and (in the case of the ARIA performance) added a new dimension to their grunge persona. The perceived authenticity associated with live music is crucial to that persona, as we'll see. These performances also demonstrate how the band created a sense of 'imagined community' (to use political scientist Benedict

Anderson's famous concept) among their audience members and with other alternative acts, especially You Am I and Radio Birdman.

Chapter 4 begins by chronicling the band's profound music development in the years following 'Tomorrow'. This is achieved via an overview of their post-*Frogstomp* albums. There is a discussion of the band's demise and the subsequent estrangement of the members. The chapter explores the influence that silverchair has had on other music acts. Much has been said about how the band's 1995 sound is indebted to other groups but little about how other groups have been indebted to silverchair.

Chapter 4 concludes by returning to *Frogstomp* and, specifically, assessing some of the ways in which the album has been remembered by music critics and silverchair members. The band may have moved quite significantly away from those beginnings, but it's clear that the 1995 record is still remembered fondly and remains a pivotal moment in Australian music. The renewed media attention to this album can be traced to a broader nostalgia for the 1990s, as well as the record's twentieth anniversary in 2015.

The book is dotted with anecdotes about my own memories of *Frogstomp*. These provide an intimate perspective on some ways that music can shape an individual's sense of self and their experience of the world. It's a cultural studies cliché that we make meaning of the pop culture we consume. I turned fifteen in 1995; *Frogstomp* is a potent reminder of the youngster I was, or wanted to be, or want to remember myself as being. Ultimately, *Frogstomp* has become an object of profound nostalgia for me, with nostalgia here manifesting as 'a yearning for a different time – the time of our childhood, the slower rhythms of our dreams' (Boym 2001: xv).

Let's remember, though, that nostalgia can distort and mislead; it can encourage false and even deceptive reflections on the ways we were. This is something that I have been mindful of; the reader is left to decide whether the tome has been penned by an author wearing rose-tinted glasses.

Further, I am mindful that a book by a whiteboy author of an album by whiteboy rockers will obscure the work of female and Aboriginal and Torres Strait Islander musicians who were performing during the mid-1990s. There is important scholarship on these artists (Bracknell and Barwick 2020; Strong and Rogers 2016); their work deserves further critical attention.

1 Grunge and generationalism from Seattle to Newcastle

This chapter explicates *Frogstomp*'s profound cultural significance by situating it within the sociohistorical moment in which it was produced. The chapter suggests that this album reflects the 'global cultural flows' of popular culture that are themselves symptomatic of globalization. *Frogstomp*-era silverchair boasted a range of international influences. Further, the chapter argues the album owes its life as much to the cultivation of an alternative youth audience in Australia as it does to Seattle grunge bands. This cultivation was being undertaken by triple j. In 2009, Ben Eltham argued that '[t]riple J is a keystone of Australian culture and a kind of strange hybrid that sits in an uncomfortable middle ground between its commercial and community radio cousins.' Eltham (2009) wrote that the station 'does some very important things, particularly in terms of its youth current affairs programming and its outreach to independent bands and regional communities, that no other Australian cultural institution even tries [to do]'. The cultivation of an alternative youth culture also came via the short-lived TV talent program *Nomad*, which was a joint initiative of triple j and government broadcaster Special

Broadcasting Service, and on which the 'chair got their big break.

Further, the chapter situates the grimness of grunge and the generational stereotypes that underpin this genre within the context of neoliberalism and economic recession. Those stereotypes are deeply problematic, but I suggest it's worth acknowledging that they also have a genesis in reality. The early 1990s, when silverchair began, was indeed a bleak socio-economic time within and outside Australia.

Grunge, alternative music and subcultural capital

'Grunge music' describes a rock sub-genre that emerged in America – and specifically Seattle – during the late 1980s and early 1990s, via the work of bands that included Nirvana, Pearl Jam, Soundgarden, Hole, Mudhoney and L7 (Attfield 2023; Strong 2013). Grunge featured several key attributes: distorted guitars, lyrics riddled with angst and ennui, and a disdain for commercialism. This anti-commercialism was sometimes interpreted by fans and media reports as a snub against the corporation-defined mainstream. Music scholar Catherine Strong writes: 'In everyday discourse, the mainstream is often connected to ideas of conformity and is also contrasted to realness, genuine creativity, independence' (2013: 76). The mainstream is here understood as a site of profound unoriginality and conformity, a place where one stays safe in order to hopefully make those big bucks.

The grunge snub against the mainstream is most famously suggested in the 1992 *Rolling Stone*[1] cover in which Kurt Cobain (flanked by his Nirvana bandmates Krist Novoselic and Dave Grohl) wears a T-shirt with the handwritten message 'Corporate Magazines Still Suck'. The message is itself a riff on the tagline of indie label SST Records, which was 'Corporate Rock Sucks' (Soulsby 2015). There is a knowing irony in that image; the band are acknowledging that there is no way of entirely situating oneself outside the profit-driven, commercial music industry of which they were critical.

Musically, grunge is indebted to punk, another genre known for its anti-authoritarianism. Australian post-punk act The Scientists influenced bands such as Mudhoney, as we'll discover later in the chapter. Grunge was also indebted to 1980s heavy metal, as well as 1970s rock; for instance, Neil Young influenced both Nirvana and Pearl Jam and recorded an album (1995's *Mirror Ball*) with members of the latter group (Taysom 2020).

A key facet of the grunge music scene was fashion. This was focused on clothing: think flannelette shirts, ripped jeans, sneakers, even the 'baby doll' attire championed by Courtney Love. Grunge fashion also meant long hair, generally unkempt and parted in the middle. This fashion can be read as a snub against the stylistic excesses of 1980s mainstream rock. Bouffant coiffures, shoulder pads and spandex pants were not, it seemed, conducive with being anti-establishment! Grunge

---

[1] The US version of *Rolling Stone* will be referred to by that title, while the Australian/New Zealand edition will be referred to as *Rolling Stone Australia/ NZ*. This is done for clarity (both magazines share very similar content).

fashion was then a way of saying 'appearance doesn't matter' – when of course it does. And, grunge fashion was a way of marking oneself as belonging to a particular 'scene', a musical community, be that as a performer, listener or both (Moore 2005: 239; Stafford 2018).

Paradoxically, grunge music was not immune to widespread appeal and marketability. As Moore (2005: 231–232) elucidates:

> Youthful expressions of alienation and rebellion can be valuable commodities. . . . Corporations and advertisers know that [the] youth market is notoriously fickle and cannot be easily manipulated through simple marketing hype, and so they try to align themselves with music, fashion, images, and celebrities that appear to young people as authentic, cutting-edge, or cool. In doing so they commercialize sounds and styles from youth cultures and marginal subcultures. (Moore 2005: 231–232)

If this process sounds familiar, then it should; in the 1970s, punk fashion – which was associated with youthful rebellion and designed to be in-your-face and most certainly not mainstream – became stocked in mainstream stores (Hebdige 1979: 96). The difference being that where the commodification of punk presaged that subculture's decline, the commodification of grunge seems to have been ongoing throughout grunge's popularity; in the wake of *Nevermind*'s success, there never seemed to be a moment that 'grunge' was not a marketable entity (whatever the intentions or personal values of the performers covered by that label). The *Rolling Stone* cover is a case in point.

The marketability of grunge was likely due to the fact that it was categorized (by media pundits, record labels) as alternative music. Alternative music is a broad and contested label, as even a cursory scan of scholarship on this topic suggests (e.g. Moore 2005; Stratton 2007b). The alternativeness of music has been gauged by factors that include whether it has been released by an independent record label; genre (e.g. grunge, punk); the extent to which the music defies the musical conventions commonly heard on commercial/mainstream radio, for example, via loud and aggressive arrangements (Stratton 2007b: 67); and whether the artists producing the music take an anti-commercial and/or anti-authoritarian stance in their work and public lives.

Importantly, for this chapter, alternative music has been imbued with subcultural capital. The term 'subcultural capital' was coined by Sarah Thornton in her 1995 study of club cultures. This refers to in-group hierarchies that distinguish high-status insiders (the 'hip') from low-status imposters (the 'poseurs') and, of course, the 'alternative' from the so-called 'mainstream' (Moore 2005: 232). Subcultural capital is premised on authenticity, this being a cultural construct that is commonly understood in the musical sense as encompassing factors such as the evocation of intimacy in one's performances and a desire to produce music that is not exclusively (or largely) driven by profit (Moore 2002: 210–2011). Bands like Nirvana certainly sought to cultivate a sense of authenticity in their public image.

The point of noting the marketability and mainstreaming of grunge is not to portray grunge musos as sell-outs or hypocrites. The point is to acknowledge that the music industry is, yes, an industry. Industries exist to generate a profit. The point is also to acknowledge that the popularity of grunge provided fertile ground for silverchair's success. silverchair admitted to being fans of, and influenced by, Pearl Jam. The boys had the grunge aesthetic down pat, with their streetwear and flowing tresses, and articulated something of a non-mainstream stance. For example, they chose Murmur (a subsidiary of Sony that operated independently) to release their debut album. Johns allegedly justified this business decision by telling his bandmates that 'if we signed straight to a big label . . . there'll be all this advertising and shit' (cited in Apter 2018: 25). Murmur was not, of course, a genuine independent, or 'indie', label, if one takes 'independent' to mean independent of 'major record companies' (Galuszka and Wyrzykowska 2019: 34).[2] Nonetheless, Johns' observation suggests how 'indie' labels were sometimes regarded within the music industry as valid alternatives to the 'centralized corporate culture' embodied by bigger labels and the rigidity and conformity that characterized that culture (Attfield 2023: 41).

Further, Johns echoed many a Seattle rocker when he declared: 'We don't want to be known as the band who think they're rock stars' (cited in Apter 2018: 32). The singer told triple j in 1995:

---

[2] Galuszka and Wyrzykowska (2019) examine the various ways in which the term 'independent label' has been understood since the 1990s.

All we want the album to do is hang around in the alternative charts in the top 20 for a while and then it can drop down and do whatever it wants. It's not that we don't want success. We just don't want to get established as a mainstream teen band, we want people to take us seriously. (cited in Tran and Wicks 2021)

These remarks may not have been entirely sincere. Gillies recalls that the band did want to 'be "big"', even if they didn't know exactly what this might entail or even expect it to happen (Gillies et al. 2023: 52). That point is moot. What's important is that they wanted to create an alternative rock star image.

Finally, my aim is to demonstrate that the boundaries separating alternative and mainstream are indeed porous. How could they not be? Alternative and mainstream are deeply subjective with two different listeners likely to give wildly different definitions of each. It could indeed be argued that grunge is an example par excellence of how alternative and mainstream converge; through being classified as alternative music, grunge acts such as silverchair could achieve mainstream success.

And while mainstream might be a dirty word for some music aficionados, that's not the case for all. Strong's 2013 study demonstrates that grunge music fans have understood how that genre intersected with the mainstream and that this intersection was not necessarily negative. One interviewee is quoted as saying that the mainstreaming of grunge 'was really good, it gave a lot of people an opportunity to hear stuff they wouldn't have heard before and it gave bands an opportunity to reach an audience they wouldn't have reached before' (cited in Strong 2013: 80). That statement resonates with me. My own interest in silverchair encouraged me to learn more about the bands that influenced and/or collaborated with them, especially You Am I. I was familiar with You Am I through their regular triple j rotation. Their duet with silverchair at the 1995 ARIA Awards (see Chapter 3 for a discussion) encouraged me to listen to more of their work, even if I never became a fan of theirs in the way I became a fan of the Newcastle rockers.

Generations, neoliberalism and recession

There is a strong generational current in media reportage of grunge music, especially *Frogstomp*-era silverchair. It's important to briefly examine this current – the form it took and whether it can enrich or detract from an appreciation of the album.

Let's start with the concept of 'generations'. This encompasses all the lived experiences of folk born during a particular set of years, from their clothing choices to their pop culture preferences and their world views. Historically, a new generation is thought to be born every thirty years. This is because, as Hungarian sociologist Karl Mannheim put it, 'during the first 30 years of life people are still learning . . . individual creativeness on an average begins only at that age, and that at 60 a man [*sic*] quits public life' (2013: 278).

The spectre of generations has certainly haunted rock music mythology. Rock music gained ascendance during the 1950s, shortly after the 'teenager' had become an identifiable social group and market sub-section. Tom Hennessey writes that 'the teenager emerged in Britain as a physical manifestation of Americanisation; an impulsive and sexually active consumer highly responsive to transatlantic trends, and expressive of certain urges habitually suppressed by the parent culture' (2023: 25). In this passage, Hennessey highlights the US origins of the teenager, which have elsewhere been acknowledged by other researchers (e.g. Savage 2007).[3] He also emphasizes a symbiotic relationship between teenagers, rock music and rebellion, particularly rebellion against one's elders.

Rock music certainly became 'the lynch pin for a number of cultural industries to organise their production lines with that consumer group in mind' (Tzioumakis and Lincoln 2019: 22). Those industries ranged from music and film to fashion. Through purchasing these products, teen consumers were effectively purchasing markers of identity, a sense of belonging in a certain rock subculture (Hebdige 1979) and a riposte to the social mores championed by their older family members.

During the 1990s, grunge music was commonly understood (at least in mainstream media) as, if not a rebellion, then definitely a mode through which GenX could talk back to their parents' generation, the Baby Boomers, who were born between 1945 and the early 1960s. According to a certain media narrative, the latter generation was especially blessed:

they were the beneficiaries of a post-war economic boom that ushered in an era of unprecedented prosperity. They

---

[3] Savage (2007: 448) identifies the 1944 launch of the fashion-oriented *Seventeen* magazine in the United States as a key moment in the development of 'the teen' as a sociological category.

became, up to that point in our history, our most highly educated generation, setting a pro-education example that subsequent generations have enthusiastically followed. They also established new records for international travel, for home ownership and for divorce. (Mackay 2024: 27)

The Boomers (to use a currently popular pejorative) had protested America's war in Vietnam and advocated for free love. But by the 1990s, according to this narrative, that generation had become politically acquiescent. Boomers, it was said, failed to understand the struggles of young people, much less appreciate their own privilege at being born into a supposedly less troubled world (Bristow 2015).

Grunge music, then, was often read as a way for GenXers to document their experiences of that world, their feelings – especially their angst. This reading is not without basis. That cohort came of age during the late twentieth century, in a world of rampant neoliberalism, which David Harvey describes as

in the first instance a theory of political economic practices that proposes that human well-being can best be advanced by liberating individual entrepreneurial freedoms and skills within an institutional framework characterized by strong private property rights, free markets, and free trade. The role of the state is to create and preserve an institutional framework appropriate to such practices. (2005: 2)

In Australia, neoliberalism flourished under the centrist Hawke-Keating Labor government, which spanned 1983–96. Political scientist Elizabeth Humphrys identifies that government's

1983 floating of the Australian dollar on the global currency market and the Accord (whereby the federal government and the Australian Council of Trade Unions[4] agreed to restrict wage inflation) as 'paradigmatic of' neoliberal reforms in this country (2018: 100).

During the late 1980s and early 1990s, a global recession impacted much of the West. This recession was ignited by a number of economic shocks, including the global stock market crash of October 1987 (Starke et al. 2013: 92). In Australia, '[u]nemployment rose sharply during 1991–1992 to over 10 per cent' (Starke et al. 2013: 100). Young people usually bear the brunt of economic downturns, and the early 1990s downturn was no exception; in 1992, the Australian youth unemployment rate peaked at over 20 per cent (Chalmers 2020). Mark Davis wrote in 1997 that

> young people are suffering. They have the highest suicide rates in [Australia]. They are most likely to be long-term unemployed. The numbers of homeless young people have risen rapidly. They have been among the main losers in cuts to government services. In Australia's new 'flexible' labour market, young people have little prospect of the job security that their parents took for granted. (viii)

This disadvantage was concealed by the hostile GenX stereotypes that were frequently reproduced by the media and will be discussed throughout this book.

---

[4] The Australian Council of Trade Unions (ACTU) is the peak body for trade unions in Australia.

Let me be clear that I am not against generational frameworks. Such frameworks can be useful in studying certain demographics, at least to a point. There are doubtless similar factors (political, social) that have shaped the lives of those born during a particular time. There may well be sociological merit in trying to assess how those factors influenced the music produced by those who belong to a specific generation.

Conversely, an uncritical emphasis on generations can homogenize the lives and work of those individuals who were born at a certain time. Reading grunge music as always and only the expression of GenX ennui elides the rich and diverse influences, images and ideas that can be detected throughout this body of music. And, it's worth remembering that '"Generation X" isn't an expression used by anyone in the age group it refers to' (Davis 1997: 15). Mark Davis makes this observation in his astute study of generation-based discourses in the 1990s Australian media. Within this media milieu, GenX were frequently talked about, generally by Boomer commentators. For those commentators, GenX spelled 'trouble' – they wore the wrong kinds of clothes and listened to the wrong kind of music (Davis 1997: 11). They were stereotyped variously as apathetic, antisocial, lazy and victim-obsessed. Davis cites a range of examples to support this argument, including crude and hostile press depictions of unemployed teenagers and student activists. Seldom did young people have their own voice to articulate their own views and experiences.

Building on that last point, we could argue that silverchair were significant as they did have a public voice. The boys from Newcastle were not always morose and moody; Chapter

3 provides examples of their wicked humour. Indeed, it's indisputable that the band members' tender years formed a key part of their appeal. After all, how many fifteen-year-olds could play with such maturity?

Oh, and the band's success puts paid to Mannheim's suggestion that one reaches their creative zenith at age thirty! His statement about public life ending at sixty is similarly dated, given the increasingly long working lives of individuals.

Finally, reading grunge as an expression of generational attitudes and lives is problematic because many of the bands labelled 'grunge' did not claim to be making sociological or political statements in their music. To cite one famous example: Nirvana's 'Smells Like Teen Spirit' (1991) has been read as a treatise on youthful malaise, when in fact the 'teen spirit' it references was actually an American deodorant (Queenan 2007)! This absence of overt political engagement distinguished grunge from punk, the latter of which has historically critiqued capitalism and the institutions that support it in a way that grungers usually did not.

Globalization and global cultural flows

In this section, I want to further tease out *Frogstomp*'s significance by situating its production within the context of globalization. This refers to a sociohistorical phenomenon in which the flow of 'people, machinery, money, images now follow increasingly nonisomorphic paths' on a global scale (Appadurai 1996: 37). There are many examples of how globalization has impacted Australian music. Think about the Japanese multinational Sony establishing ties in Australia via Sony Music Australia. The latter hosted Murmur, the record label that released *Frogstomp*. Think about Australian acts ranging from Peter Allen to Kylie Minogue, Helen Reddy and INXS making it big in Britain and America.

This chapter focuses specifically on globalization's transnational cultural flows. As postcolonial theorist Arjun Appadurai (1996) points out, these flows gathered pace during the late twentieth century, thanks to factors that include increasingly sophisticated technological advances – from the television set and VCR to the World Wide Web. Appadurai argued that during a time of global cultural flows, North America 'is no longer the puppeteer of a world system of images but is only one node of a complex transnational construction of imaginary landscapes' (1996: 37). To take the example of Australian music: there is no denying that certain bands and trends have American influences, but their work is also indebted to specifically Australian actors and institutions. And those American influences are themselves shaped by global cultural flows.

Let's elaborate on that last point with reference to grunge itself. Australian singer, composer and bandleader Kim Salmon has remarked that 'Australian music was the premier exporter of grunge' and there are some important reasons for this (cited in Stratton 2007a: 146). Salmon's band The Scientists has been cited as a key influence on Mudhoney's music by that band's lead singer, Mark Arm, with other influences being the US acts Neil Young and The Stooges (Stratton 2007a: 146). The word 'grunge' might have its genesis as US 1960s slang and may be most commonly associated with Seattle rockers, but Salmon claims that he used the term 'grunge' in 1983 to describe The Scientists sound (Stratton 2007a: 165). Salmon recalls that he used this term during an interview with triple j, which played a pivotal role in launching silverchair's career.

Indeed, a 2016 study points out that numerous US grunge artists have appreciated and even been influenced by Australian rock acts (Strong and Rogers 2016: 42). Pearl Jam guitarist Mike McCready has remarked: 'I grew up on [The Angels 'albums] *No Exit* and *Night Attack*.[5] That is the Australian music that meant so much to me, maybe because me and my friends were the only ones who knew them' (cited in Davies 2014). Guns N' Roses were also influenced by The Angels, with the former performing The Angels' song 'Marseilles' at a Las Vegas concert as a tribute to that band's lead singer, Doc Neeson, upon his death in 2014 (Baroni 2014). Bassist Ross Knight recalls his band, The Cosmic Psychos, 'hanging out' with Nirvana, with whom they shared a producer (Butch Vig) (cited in Burke and Egan 2020). A 1992 *Rolling Stone* profile on Kurt Cobain reveals that The Cosmic Psychos were among the bands in the music collection that Cobain shared with wife Courtney Love (Azerrad 1992; Strong and Rogers 2016: 43).

So, framing the origins of the grunge phenomenon as being unique to North America is problematic. In an era of global cultural flows, pop culture trends and movements can move rapidly between nations and cultures, shaping and being reshaped by the specificities (geographic, artistic) of

---

[5]The Angels were a hugely popular Oz Rock band whose hits included 'Am I Ever Gonna See Your Face Again' (1977) and 'No Secrets' (1980).

each new setting. The grunge music of early 1980s Australia may well have influenced the more globally famous grunge music of late 1980s to early 1990s Seattle, which, in turn, would influence mid-1990s grunge bands that were located within and outside America.

Nomad, triple j and Australian alternative music

If you run a Google search for the television program *Nomad*, only a smattering of relevant results will emerge. The show aired on SBS for one year from May 1993 and lived up to its title by 'wander[ing] through all the diverse aspects of music, art and dance' (cited in Lang 1993: 38). This was an ambitious effort and one that seems to have largely vanished from public view.

The few online references to *Nomad* almost exclusively mention silverchair and with good reason – the then Innocent Criminals had their big break when their tape recording of 'Tomorrow' was selected from 800 entries for that show's 'Pick Me' competition. The competition sought 'the best demo recording by an unsigned Australian band' (Apter 2018: 17). One of the judges, British video director Robert Hambling, remarked that the band's signature tune 'had all of those things you want out of a great song . . . Memorable lyrics, a really good hook. And there was no denying their connection to the Seattle sound' (cited in Apter 2018: 17). Hambling was surprised that the three purveyors of that sound were not yet of legal drinking age (which, in Australia, was eighteen years in 1994 and remains the case; see Makkai and McAllister 1998).

The 'Pick Me' prizes included the opportunity to film a music video for 'Tomorrow' and to record an extended play (EP) at a Sydney studio for triple j, with whom *Nomad* had run the competition. triple j has been Australia's best-known proponent of alternative music. To understand how this status came to be, let's turn back the clock to 1975 when the station emerged under the name '2JJ', or Double Jay, on the AM band. The station quickly became associated with playing Australian content and bucking the constraints of the mainstream; for example, 2JJ launched itself by playing Skyhooks' ostensibly (though not in actuality) banned song 'You Just Like Me Cos I'm Good in Bed' (Albury 1999: 55). The station hosted discussions of controversial topics such as sex (triple j 2015a).

triple j also targeted a demographic that was both youthful and whose musical tastes were not well catered to by other radio stations. For instance, they played the Sydney group Radio Birdman, who were heavily influenced by US alternative acts such as The Stooges and whose music sat somewhere between punk and the harder end of Oz Rock. Birdman's classic song 'New Race' would be covered by silverchair at 1995's ARIA Awards (see Chapter 3).

Fast-forward to the late 1980s and the station – now known as 2JJJ or triple j and operating on the FM band – underwent a radical transformation. Until that point, triple j was broadcast exclusively in Sydney. However, Peter Loxton (at the time the Controller of Metropolitan and Regional Radio and 2JJJ) felt that 'networking was an access and equity issue: if Triple J was a good youth service, all Australians should have access to it. If it wasn't, the ABC should not support it at all' (Albury 1999: 56). The ABC is funded by taxpayers around the country, and yet at this time, triple j could only be heard by listeners based in Sydney's inner city.

Thus, in October 1989, triple j started a gradual roll-out of broadcasting to other major Australian cities and to Newcastle. Earlier that year, in March, the station ran a special event known as the Hot 100, whereby listeners could write in with a list of their ten favourite songs of all time (triple j 2015b). The Hot 100 was unexpectedly popular and became a yearly staple, eventually being renamed Hottest 100 and playing tunes that enjoyed a high rotation on that station throughout the prior twelve months.

So, by the mid-1990s, triple j had two key strengths. First, it had helped cultivate what historian Michelle Arrow calls 'a new imagined community of youth across the nation' (2009: 144).[6] Second, the station appeared to bestow a sense of subcultural capital to listeners. This capital suffused everything associated with the station, from its drum logo to the music played; in 1999, Kath Albury wrote that 'sales of CDs rise "substantially" when they are added to the [station's] playlist' (59). So, much like grunge itself, triple j helped bring alternative

At this point, I'll need to get personal. Back in the mid-1990s, I was unfamiliar with the term 'subcultural capital', and yet this was absolutely what drove me to champion triple j to whomever would listen. As I remarked circa 1995: 'I like triple j because they don't play Top 40 bullshit.' I couldn't quite articulate what it was about this 'Top 40 bullshit' that I didn't like. Perhaps, on reflection, I fell into the trap of assuming that

____

[6]The concept of 'imagined communities' will be explored at greater length in Chapter 3.

those who listened to popular music – or, at least, popular music that didn't surface on triple j – were unthinkingly conforming to broader societal expectations of what you should like and what you should listen to.

Never mind that grunge music was being played on even 'mainstream' commercial radio stations and promoted on the covers of 'corporate magazines'!

silverchair's global cultural flows

silverchair began life as Innocent Criminals in 1992. The band comprised Daniel Johns on vocals and guitars, Chris Joannou on bass guitar and Ben Gillies on drums. There was initially a fourth member, rhythm guitarist Tobin Finnane, but he departed in 1994 to live overseas for a time with his family. The members met at school and started practising their craft in bedrooms, garages and classrooms. The friendship between the boys was as much a driver of the band in its early days as any dreams of stardom. Gillies recalled that the band members 'were more than friends, more than bandmates, we were brothers' (Gillies et al. 2023: 53).

The boys were not from families who were working in the music industry nor were they even familiar with that industry prior to their kids' success. They were working-class folk who were deeply invested in the boys' musical passion, as Chapter 2 discusses. Gillies would remember: 'My childhood was pretty stock standard. . . . Life, for me, revolved around sport, the beach, my mates and music' (Gillies et al. 2023: 10–11). If this beginning sounds unremarkable, then it absolutely is.

This is surely what gave silverchair a sense of relatability. That modesty and relatability were increased by their being located not in a capital city but in a traditionally working-class regional city. And it's a city that, as we saw in the Introduction, is not famous for its music scene.

Yet, in saying that, it's worth noting that Newcastle has a particularly rich musical history. An assortment of choirs, bands and singing groups have formed in the city since the early nineteenth century (English et al. 2018). Rock band Velvet Underground (not to be confused with the US group of the same name) began in Newcastle in 1967 and ran until 1972; its members included Australian rock luminaries such as Malcolm Young (later of AC/DC) and Les Hall (who would go on to become guitarist in Les Mulry Gang) (Kimbo 2015). The Newcastle electronic music group Nasenbluten formed in 1992 and gained a considerable following on account of their 'D.I.Y. approach and punk attitude' (Rodriguez 2014). Their name translates to English as 'nosebleed', which hints at their hard-hitting image. Nasenbluten's music was released through their own label, the vividly named Bloody Fist Productions, which they established (in 1994) after no other company would take them on. The band were performing at roughly the same historical moment as silverchair were developing their music.

In terms of music venues, The Star Hotel was extremely popular during the 1970s; its 1979 closure inspired riots in the streets, which were immortalized in Cold Chisel's 1980 track 'Star Hotel' (Anthony and Millington 2019). Newcastle was also home to The Cambridge Hotel, which operated from 1958 to

2023. The Cambridge hosted bands such as silverchair and The Screaming Jets, the latter of whom rose to popularity in Australia during the early 1990s. silverchair were an opening act for The Screaming Jets in 1994 (Fricke 1996; Newstead 2023).

Both The Screaming Jets and Velvet Underground were aligned with the pub rock tradition, which Daniel Johns recalls being particularly popular in the Newcastle he grew up in (Johns 2021: Episode 2). As its name suggests, pub rock centres around rock music played in pubs and other alcohol-oriented venues. This genre gained ascendance during the late 1960s (when licenced gigs were introduced in Australia) and ran until at least the early 1990s, 'when alternative music from the inner cities became the dominant form' (Oldham 2024; unpaginated). Paul Oldham's 2013 study demonstrates that pub rock's audiences were mostly male and working class. This might help explain the genre's popularity in Newcastle, a city replete with mines and factories, sites that have historically been 'where hegemonic masculinity[7] is continually and aggressively reasserted and reproduced' (Winchester 1999: 84). This masculinity was another defining feature of the city, having been satirized in Bob Hudson's popular 1975 track 'The Newcastle Song'.

That loud and aggressive sound has also been a characteristic feature of what is sometimes called 'Australian Rock', or 'Oz Rock'. Oz Rock is a genre that emerged from pub

---

[7]The concept of 'hegemonic masculinity' was popularized by Australian sociologist Raewyn Connell (2005), who used it to describe performances of masculinity characterized by physical strength and acts of dominance (sexual, emotional) over women.

rock and that encompasses a host of 'mainstream, mass-marketed, identifiably Australian' acts (Rhodes and Pullen 2012: 33–34). silverchair were fans of popular Oz Rock bands Cold Chisel and Baby Animals; the latter band's eponymous 1991 debut album was actually engineered by Kevin Shirley, who (as the following chapter discusses) would produce *Frogstomp*. They would be indebted to Oz Rock in other ways, too, as we'll see throughout the book.

Additionally, silverchair were indebted to other musical influences from around the Western world. Their playlists included Pearl Jam and Soundgarden and the British groups Led Zeppelin and Black Sabbath (Turnman 1995). Podcaster Daniel Hedger (2020) has observed that the guitar riff from *Frogstomp*'s 'Leave Me Out' resembles that of Black Sabbath's 'Sweet Leaf' (1971). Ben Gillies has reminisced about finding a videocassette recording of Zeppelin's 1973 Madison Square Garden concert and 'watch[ing] it like I was studying for a test' (Gillies et al. 2023: 37).

It's worth pausing (as it were) on that last anecdote. The videocassette recorder (VCR) emerged as part of the 'technological explosion' that Appadurai mentions, materializing with increased frequency in households across the world during the 1980s (1996: 29). VCRs were revolutionary technology during this time because they allowed viewers to consume celluloid entertainment in their own homes, as opposed to more public spaces such as cinemas. In the VCR era, cultural texts – films, television shows, concerts – that might otherwise have been consigned to history were now preserved for regular viewing. And so it was that this medium brought the work of an English group rocking out in a US stadium to a Newcastle youngster – though in fairness, Gillies had been introduced to that band earlier by his father.

The Innocent Criminals cut their teeth playing at local pubs and in a Newcastle Mall talent competition (Gillies et al. 2023: 38–40). Their first television appearance came in 1993, when they thrashed out their tune 'I Felt Like It' on Newcastle television station NBN. There exists grainy YouTube footage of this performance. The show begins with a cherubic, braces-wearing Johns declaring, 'let's rock 'n' roll!' before breaking into song, his notorious deep-voiced growl not yet intact. Occasionally, the band looked to their surrounds for musical inspiration; 'Faultline', a track which appears on *Frogstomp* and which we'll discuss in Chapter 2, is one example.

In 1994, two quintessentially twentieth-century technological innovations – television and radio – would transport Innocent Criminals to a national and then an international audience.

Summing-up

This chapter has argued that in order to fully appreciate *Frogstomp*'s cultural significance, it's critical to situate its genesis within the specific sociohistorical milieu of 1990s Australia. This was a time of neoliberalism and economic strife, the latter of which was doubtless a factor influencing the construction of the angst-ridden GenX stereotypes. Grunge music has been understood (rightly or otherwise) as a cultural expression par excellence of that angst.

The 1990s was also a time of globalization and its attendant 'global cultural flows' of culture. Yes, silverchair borrowed from the Seattle grunge scene, both musically and aesthetically, but their music also had distinct Australian and British influences. The band would never have achieved success had it not been for triple j, which had been busily (re-)modelling itself as a hub for alternative

2 *Frogstomp*, the album

This chapter opens by discussing the production of *Frogstomp*. We move on to describe each of the album's eleven tracks. This is necessary in highlighting the album's lyrical and emotional diversity. The chapter then explores silverchair's promotion of their record and their achievement of commercial success. There is a discussion of the band's enthusiastic fans and the sometimes quite unsettling interactions between Daniel Johns and certain devotees. The chapter concludes with an overview of the album's critical reception, whereby reviewers noted its derivativeness and the band's youth while applauding silverchair's raw talent.

Innocent Criminals no longer

Before addressing *Frogstomp* itself, it's worth briefly addressing the band's rebranding. In late 1994, Innocent Criminals became silverchair. The inspiration for this new name has been the source of conjecture. Perhaps the boys were inspired by C. S. Lewis' classic 1953 fantasy novel *The Silver Chair*. Or perhaps it was a mash-up of You Am I's 'Berlin Chair' (1993) and Nirvana's 'Sliver' (1992). The mash-up story, Gillies and Joannou would later concede, was a 'piss-take' (Gillies et al. 2023: 61). Neither could recall if the Lewis book ever entered their consciousness.

Gillies and Joannou did remember that they wanted to move away from Innocent Criminals because, as they put it, '[t]hat was the name of a kids' band, and we weren't kids anymore. Or so we thought' (Gillies et al. 2023: 61).

The infantilism of Innocent Criminals remains debatable; let's not forget blues-reggae act Ben Harper and the Innocent Criminals. The difference is that that band was formed (in the late 1990s) by Harper when he was in his twenties; the silverchair boys were, in 1994, still teenagers. They wanted to deflect attention from this, even if this meant assuming a moniker that could have been inspired by a kids' book. This desire to distance oneself from the naivete of youth, and be taken seriously, is one that would follow silverchair, and especially Johns, for years to come.

Recording *Frogstomp*

Working on an album was all we'd ever wanted to do.

Thus recalled Ben Gillies in *Love and Pain* (Gillies et al. 2023: 78). The band had experience in the recording studio. silverchair had produced an Extended Play as part of their *Nomad* prize. This EP was released in September 1994 and comprised four tracks: the breakthrough hit 'Tomorrow', as well as 'Stoned', 'Blind' and 'Acid Rain' (Gillies et al. 2023: 57). Later that year, the band was ready to move from EP to LP (long play).

Frogstomp was recorded over nine days in December 1994–January 1995, in Sydney's Festival Studios, at a cost of approximately only $30,000 (Gillies et al. 2023: 96). The album was produced by Johannesburg-born Kevin 'Caveman' Shirley, who had been invited onto the project by the director of A&R and International Marketing at Sony, John Watson. In 2021, Watson recalled that he felt Shirley 'was one of the only people in Australia that could make this record' (Johns 2021: Episode 3). Shirley could work quickly, which was crucial given the limited teenage attention spans he would be harnessing. Shirley was also 'sonically raw and loud', says Watson, and was himself a 'big kid . . . so he was totally on their wavelength' (Johns 2021: Episode 3). Gillies and Joannou would write in 2023: 'Kevin's sound is distinctive. There's an energy and a rawness to his work' (Gillies et al. 2023: 43). Shirley's talent would see him sought after in the years that followed by acts ranging from Perth alternative rock band Ammonia to US stadium-fillers Aerosmith and British heavy metal act Iron Maiden. Shirley would recall that Maiden wanted to work with him because they 'loved' *Frogstomp*'s sound (cited in McNeice 2010).

Happily, Shirley shepherded the album through to completion in a speedy time.

This effort can doubtless be attributed to a combination of efficient working and Shirley's own musical smarts. While Watson talks of Shirley being a 'big kid', Shirley himself recalls the benefits of his performing the role of 'rebel schoolteacher' (Apter 2018: 41). He'd allow the band the opportunity to race around furiously in the studio corridors, pushing a trolley, but he wasn't afraid to bring them back into line with a stern 'Right, we need you now' (Apter 2018: 41). And the silverchair boys could follow instructions. For instance, Gillies and Joannou recall Shirley telling them at one point: 'You need a fast, heavy song' (2023: 76). The band responded by bashing out 'Madman' in around twenty minutes.

Indeed, Shirley felt similarly affirmative towards silverchair. In 1996, he would say: 'The alarming thing is that the guys sound as mature as they do . . . You can definitely hear the influences. But they weren't embarrassed about showing those influences' (cited in Apter 2018: 43).

Frogstomp was released by Murmur, which was chosen in part because it was not a huge corporate behemoth – though, of course, it was part of a multinational corporation. The band's decision to sign with this label was also influenced by their camaraderie with the men they came to know affectionately as 'the two Johns'. These were John O'Donnell, the head of Murmur, and John Watson (Gillies et al. 2023: 64). Both men spotted the band's talent early on and nurtured it accordingly. Gillies has written: 'We were kids and they recognised that, but they still respected us as musicians' (Gillies et al. 2023: 64–65). Compare this with the suggestion from some *Frogstomp* reviewers, which will be discussed later in the chapter, that 'kids' couldn't produce great music.

In 2021, Watson recalled being excited about silverchair after learning about their triple j recording session and subsequently travelling to Newcastle to watch one of their live shows:

I've still got the set list and it's the most extraordinary thing, you know, that you could ever imagine seeing. That was always our belief that, you know, if they're capable of doing this at 15, imagine what they'll do at 25 if they just give them the chance. (Johns 2021: Episode 2)

Watson would soon leave Sony to become the band's manager, a position he held until their 2011 break-up. This career move demonstrates a powerful faith in silverchair and their future; previously, Watson only had experience managing his own band (Graham 2019: 63). The experience of managing silverchair was, in turn, the catalyst for even bolder career moves. In 2000, he launched the recording label Eleven, which would release the chair's final two albums, *Diorama* (2002) and *Young Modern* (2007) (see Chapter 4 for a discussion of both).

So, let's now turn to *Frogstomp* itself. But before we do that, let's talk about the rather, shall we say, unique name. 'Frogstomp' was lifted from US saxophonist and band leader Floyd Newman's 1963 'Frog Stomp'. The upbeat, bluesy beat of that track sounds a million miles from the record under discussion here (Hedger 2020). Though perhaps the lack of sonic resemblance is beside the point. So, too, may be a familiarity with Newman's record. The point is perhaps that *Frogstomp* is indeed a striking title and that strikingness lies in its oxymoronic nature; frogs don't stomp, do they? The wide-eyed amphibian on the album's cover could be an exception to that rule. Also, the title seems appropriate given the stomping nature of the music contained therein.

Listening to *Frogstomp*

Frogstomp begins with 'Israel's Son', which became the album's third single. The track kicks into motion with the low growl of Joannou's bass guitar. The tempo escalates when Gillies starts pounding the drums at 0.15, and the bass begins a driving riff at 0.20. Johns' baritone vocals smash through the wall of sound as he declares that he hates the listener and wants 'you' dead. He follows this up by insisting that if 'you' do not materialize quickly, he will slay your friend.

With its wrathful lyrics and thrashing beat, 'Israel's Son' sounds like a prototype of a grunge anthem. The listener can imagine the band members banging their long-haired heads and indeed that's exactly what transpires in the accompanying music video. Yet, the track is striking on two counts. The first is the enmity that pulses (lyrically and sonically) throughout the song. Who is the 'you' addressed by Johns, and why the homicidal hatred directed towards them? Who or what is the 'Israel' in the title? An evil, omnipotent overlord or someone/something else? Could the song be a reference to Middle Eastern politics (this ran through my mind as I listened to it again in 2023, with the long-running and volatile Israel–Palestine conflict making headlines)? The band provides no definitive answers and that only amplifies the track's potency.

'Israel's Son' is also striking because of the change of pace in the final forty seconds. The guitar and drums speed up. Johns' vocals grow louder, encouraging listeners to throw their hands into the air. That line could have strayed in from a dance tune; it sounds unusual and yet strangely at home on such a pounding rocker. The slow-fast, quiet-soft shifts reappear frequently on the tracks that follow.

No discussion of 'Israel's Son' would be complete without reference to the minor controversy it generated. In January 1996, a lawyer acting on behalf of a murdered US couple apportioned blame to the silverchair tune; the killers (the couple's son and an accomplice) allegedly danced to the song after the killing.

The band released a public statement distancing themselves from the 'horrific crime', and the judge exonerated them (Talbot 1996: 3). Johns has since revealed that he found the crime 'devastating' and that at the time he felt unable to publicly acknowledge this devastation (cited in Mrad 2022).

Track two is 'Tomorrow', with its familiar guitar opener and Johns navigating listeners on an expedition through a dingy town dotted with rundown properties. The singer signals early on his awareness that the listener 'hates' him. Gone, though, are the death threats and unhealable pain of 'Israel's Son'. Johns challenges his foe to 'wait till tomorrow', when presumably they/we learn that we cannot continue living luxuriously – while proclaiming that cash 'isn't everything'. The song thus seems to be turning its nose up at hypocrisy and reminding listeners not to take material comfort for granted. Unsurprisingly, the tune was inspired by a television documentary that Johns watched about an encounter between a rich man and a poor man (Apter 2018: 44).

There is another, altogether bleaker, interpretation of this tune that becomes apparent if one reads it as symptomatic of the dystopian vision of the world that circulated within mid-to-late 1990s pop culture. A new century was only a few years away, and this brought with it celebrations as well as anxieties about what was to come. Those anxieties were played out in everything from Hollywood movies like *Strange Days* (1995) to whispers about Y2K (Goodwin 2018).[1] The 'tomorrow' that

---

[1] Y2K was the name commonly assigned to a bug that would supposedly destroy computer systems globally on 1 January 2000. Happily, this bug never materialized.

Johns anticipates may not just be a time when that (boomer) capitalist is forced to eat humble pie. This 'tomorrow' might be when we're all forced to live in apocalyptic squalor.

Track 3, 'Faultline', is more sombre than the first two. The song was inspired by the 1989 Newcastle earthquake and a child who had been killed in this disaster. The pace is snail-like, with a grinding wall of guitars and drums during the choruses. Johns' plaintive vocals grow in volume as he despairs about never seeing the boy alive. The sense of finality dissipates, and a faint optimism arises in the track's concluding moments when the singer contemplates the possibility of that boy being reborn, somehow and somewhere. The guitars and drumming gather pace, as if anticipating the triumphant rebirth of the fallen child.

Track 4 is 'Pure Massacre', which became the album's second single in Australia. The song opens with the pounding of drums and guitars and Johns snarling about senseless deaths. The band then transports listeners through a combat zone riddled with gunfire, terror and death. Thematically, the song is similar to 'Israel's Son' in its depiction of senseless carnage. The soft-loud shifts – while hardly innovative – amplify the emotional intensity.

Track 5, 'Shade', was the album's fourth single and returns to the melancholy territory traversed by 'Faultline'. The piece opens with a slow guitar riff, followed by Johns gently encouraging listeners to talk to somebody if they are feeling poorly. This sentiment might seem mawkish, a castaway from a stock-standard self-help book, but it marks a significant departure from the previous diatribe about mass killings.

Johns' vocals have the same tender vulnerability that we heard earlier in his tribute to the earthquake victim.

And like 'Faultline', there is no wallowing in despair; the singer reminds us not to hide in the shade, to find someone who can give you the help you need. The thrashing guitars and screamed lyrics at the conclusion – as well as representing a change of pace – seem almost cathartic; there is the sense of the band purging the grief and sorrow that they've just chronicled.

Track 6, 'Leave Me Out', begins in grand style with pounding drums and that Black Sabbath-esque guitar riff. The track continues at a rollicking pace, with Johns enthusiastically repeating the title lyrics. We're never told what he wishes to be left out of, only that this choice means taking the high moral road.

Track 7 is 'Suicidal Dream', a disarmingly frank (if none too subtle) account of personal demons. The importance of seeking support, so movingly invoked in 'Shade', reappears in the singer's insistence that he will kill himself by simply holding his breath The track is a slow burn musically, perhaps the closest thing on the album to a ballad, before speeding up to a wall of sound climax. Johns' matter-of-fact vocal delivery accentuates the disturbing nature of the lyrics.

Track 8 is 'Madman', a thrashing rocker in the headbanger style. The guitars and drums go into glorious overdrive, with lyrics restricted to a grunt and an indecipherable final line. This is a tune made for jamming and revving up the listener. And revving up may be exactly what's needed after the melancholy of 'Suicidal Dream'.

Track 9 is 'Undecided', which traverses the terrain of inter-family conflict. Our chief protagonist is a nameless daughter caught in the crossfire of a marital breakdown. Johns' vocals are frequently concealed amidst a cacophony of guitars and drums, and this nicely invokes the confusion and overwhelm experienced by the protagonist. 'Undecided' is unrelated to the 1967 song of the same name by Australian rock band The Masters Apprentices, though silverchair would include a cover of that earlier track as a B-side on 1997's 'Abuse Me' single.

Track 10, 'Cicada', revisits the world of youthful malaise, with Johns leading the listener from the tranquil naïveté of early childhood to the emotional quagmire of adolescence. Again, Johns urges listeners not to ignore pain or challenge; he likens coming of age to a 'civil war' and urges listeners not to ignore this challenge. This is the closest the album comes to making a statement on the lived experiences of young people. The message is unambiguously positive: being a teenager is tough, but it's tough for everyone, so hang in there!

Musically, 'Cicada' unfolds at a rollicking pace. This changes in the final moments, with a quiet drum solo followed by the sound of laughter and a male voice saying: 'Okay let's do it again, from the top.' This line lends the track a sense of rough authenticity (has the band been caught unawares?) and provides a reprieve from the conflict-ridden lyrics.

Track 11, 'Findaway', is the most fast-paced and upbeat on the album. The song opens with the thrashing drums of producer Kevin's son, Josh, who would make a memorable appearance at the 1995 ARIA Awards. Johns' vocals soar above the instrumentals as he chronicles the woes of a downtrodden protagonist, including drug addiction and incarceration. All is not lost, though, with Johns insisting that a way forward will be found. An album that opened with visceral intimations of hatred and carnage thus concludes on a hopeful note; no matter the bad life choices and bad thoughts, there's always the possibility of 'breaking free'.

Time for a debrief

I revisited the eleven *Frogstomp* tracks in 2023, after many years. Listening to them again left my head spinning. What the hell did I just hear? How exactly did those teenagers compile an album that plumbs the depths of human misery? What did the silverchair boys know about this misery? Were they trying to covertly (or not so covertly) tell the listener something?

Questions. So many questions.

There are no definitive answers, alas, only speculations. The band definitely took inspiration from external events, including news reports: 'Tomorrow' and 'Faultline' are examples. It's a bit of a stretch, though, to suggest that the album as a whole provides any kind of meaningful social critique.

It's not difficult to read *Frogstomp* as a kind of indirect commentary on the band members' experience of growing up in Newcastle. Joannou concedes that the band had 'seen enough' violence in that city (Gillies et al. 2023: 116). Johns has said that the Newcastle of his youth was 'renowned as being one of the toughest [cities] in the country', an environment in which he was at the very least mildly intimidated' (Johns 2021: Episode 2). Johns does not spell out who or what he found intimidating; one answer might be the strong current of hypermasculinity that Gillies has elsewhere talked about witnessing (Grynberg 2023).

The band has not admitted whether the album was ever 'about' Newcastle in any sense. Nor have they disclosed whether any of the tracks chronicled their own personal demons. Johns was credited as the songwriter on most of *Frogstomp*'s songs and has said: 'I don't try and write lyrics about me' (cited in Apter 2018: 44). It's awfully tempting to read the lyrics in light of the mental health struggles that Johns and Gillies would later open up publicly about. Again, there's no concrete evidence to suggest that this is so.

What's certain is that such tracks performed by musos so young only make them more unsettling, even decades later. Or perhaps my response says more about Adult Jay and about certain stereotypes of what young people should be like than it does about silverchair. The young people of 1995 were not shielded from the world's bleakness – that could be witnessed on the nightly news and in videos rented from the local store. The silverchair boys admitted to seeing some bleak stuff in their everyday lives growing up. Hell, bleakness was stock in trade for the grunge so many of us 1990s teens imbibed.

And no, 1990s Jay didn't find *Frogstomp* disturbing. Exhilarating, yes, and morose in places, but not disturbing.

In 2021, John Watson recalled that each silverchair album had its own theme, and that *Frogstomp*'s theme was 'innocence' (Hedger 2021). This provides an interesting way of approaching the album's contents. The band formerly known as Innocent Criminals were teenagers who'd barely left regional Newcastle when they achieved sudden worldwide success. The theme of innocence lost animates the lyrics of several songs – think

'Faultline' or 'Cicada' – and might, dare I say, describe the band's own personal trajectories. The album's tonal shift from despair to something resembling hope suggests that losing one's innocence can indeed be a rollercoaster ride.

That rollercoaster would continue in the years that followed.

Commercial success

The world that *Frogstomp* was released into was very different from the one in which this book has been written. That was a world without streaming platforms or social media. There was a World Wide Web in 1995, but it was a great deal less comprehensive and sophisticated than the eclectic, interactive online world of today. Commercial success was evaluated by the following means: promotional activities, charts, sales and fandom. The following section evaluates *Frogstomp*'s performance in each of these.

Promotional activities

Frogstomp's commercial success benefited from a savvy promotional campaign. This campaign suggests a desire on behalf of the band to stay true to their alternative image. First, there was a minimal (one week) television advertising campaign for the album, and this only happened in late 1995 due to 'pressure from Sony executives' (Apter 2018: 42). That was a bold move, given how significant the medium of television was for advertising in Australia during the late twentieth century. It was a doubly bold move when you consider the smallness of the country's TV industry. There were only three national commercial television stations in Australia in 1995, as well as Foxtel, a pay television service that launched that year (Apter 2018: 48). In terms of the government-funded stations, advertising was not shown on the ABC and only minimally on SBS (Shoebridge 1995).

The band did give media interviews, but these were carefully chosen and not plentiful. Gillies recalls:

> The Two Johns didn't force us to do interviews with the tabloid magazines or the teen-girl bible at the time, *Dolly*, because they knew we would've hated it. They also knew it was a bad career move. Instead, they set up interviews with surf mags and serious publications. They didn't try to style us and encouraged us to keep wearing our uniform of music T-shirts from our favourite bands, like You Am I, The Offspring and Mudhoney. (Gillies et al. 2023: 80)

Gillies' recollection is troubling as it reflects the persistent devaluation of female teenage music listeners and their interests. The silverchair boys were clearly aligning themselves with the 'serious' and masculinist world of Oz Rock.[2] That alignment would not have been enhanced by having one's poster being displayed on a teenage girl's bedroom wall.

Nonetheless, the band's refusal to 'talk about our celebrity crushes and embarrassing habits with a Dolly editor' (Gillies et al. 2023: 80) at least meant that they were not giving their critics further fuel for condescension. I write 'further' because

---

[2] Rhodes and Pullen (2012) provide an incisive analysis of this masculinism.

their youthfulness was already being used for disparaging purposes. Gillies has speculated that a refusal to grant too many interviews could have made the band 'even more interesting to the press. It was like the more they couldn't have us, the more they wanted us' (Gillies et al. 2023: 80).

In 1995, I could speak for hours about the private lives of Kurt Cobain and Courtney Love, or at least what was printed in gossip mags, but very little about the talented trio from Newcastle.

When the band did grant interviews, the results were not always insightful, at least when the frontman was being grilled. Simon McKenzie recalled that 'it was hard to get much more than a sentence out of [Johns]: the combined result of shyness with simple teenage introspection' (2010: 223). In a 1995 television interview with Canada's MuchMusic, for instance, Johns provides monosyllabic responses to several questions and appears nervous, playing with his hair and giggling. His responses sometimes verge on the ridiculous. For instance, when the reporter quizzes him about the references to llamas in the *Frogstomp* CD liner notes, he replies that 'they're the best animals in the world . . . cos they look so dumb'. The band did no interviews for Australian TV during 1995 to avoid exactly that kind of exchange (Hedger 2021).

Of course, the reality was that the silverchair members were not experienced in either celebrity or in life. They were simultaneously balancing the trials and tribulations of growing up with sudden international notoriety, the kind of which relatively few bands – teenage or otherwise – will ever experience. As Gillies would point out years later: 'There isn't a guidebook for dealing with fame as a teenager. It wasn't a

normal situation but it wasn't abnormal for us. It was our life'
(Gillies et al. 2023: 94).

Charts

Frogstomp achieved its greatest success easily on the Australian and American music charts. These charts are the focus of this section.

In Australia, the album was released on 27 March 1995 and became 'the first debut album by an Australian act to chart at number one [on the ARIA chart] in its first week' (Apter 2018: 42). In an era before music streaming, the ARIA chart was a key predictor of 'commercial success in both the recorded music and live music industries' (Morrow and Beckett 2022: 239). This early triumph anticipated the band's gains at that year's ARIA Awards, which were held in October and will be discussed in the following chapter.

Also, in March 1995, an American backpacker around Australia posted a 'Tomorrow' CD to a relative who was interning at radio station 89X in Detroit. That station has been credited as the first one to play that track in America (Gillies et al. 2023: 84). Around the same time, the chief programmer for Atlanta's 99X radio station, Brian Phillips, was travelling in Australia and heard silverchair's breakthrough hit. Within one week of being added to the 99X playlist, 'Tomorrow' had become 'one of the top five songs requested by listeners' (Apter 2018: 47).

Frogstomp was released in America on 20 June 1995 through the Epic label and was certified platinum on 11 September that year (Apter 2018: 56). This platinum status coincided with the band's first American tour, as Chapter 3 discusses. The album spent forty-eight weeks on the Billboard 200 chart, peaking at number nine (Billboard). 'Tomorrow' became 'the most heavily played song on US modern-rock radio stations' in 1995 (Shoebridge 1996).

When explaining why the album enjoyed such profound popularity, several factors come to mind. These include the support the band received from SBS and triple j in Australia and 99X in America. They include the Seattle influence, with Epic executive David Massey opining: 'It's a really American sound' (cited in Apter 2018: 55). Daniel Johns' biographer, Jeff Apter, points out that many of the US grunge bands were out of action circa 1995:

> Nirvana was toast when Kurt Cobain killed himself in 1994; grunge giants Pearl Jam were off the road, immersed in a legal battle with Ticketmaster over concert prices, while both Smashing Pumpkins and Soundgarden had retreated to the studio. (2018: 55)

The silverchair members could never have foreseen this void opening up, but their first album and subsequent American visits suggested they were more than willing to fill it.

silverchair's American success was particularly impressive given that historically, Australian acts have struggled to make a dent in this market. One writer puts it thus: 'The history of Australian music is littered with big-name domestic acts that have left these shores with gig bags full for high hopes only to return months later with their tails between their legs' (Holder 2005). There have been some exceptions: Little River Band, Olivia Newton John and INXS (Apter 2013). In 1995, silverchair would join the ranks of those acts. The band's ascent in the United States is remarkable for other reasons, too, as John Watson told a podcast in 2021:

> silverchair are a really odd band in America. Cos most international artists happen in the blue [Democrat] states. They happen on the coasts. The Oasises of this world of the world were huge in LA, San Francisco, New York, DC, Philly . . . silverchair were the opposite. They broke out of the heartland . . . Atlanta, Detroit, Chicago . . . New York and LA were almost the last to the party. ('Too Much and Not Enough', Episode 17)

The success in Atlanta and Detroit is perhaps unsurprising, given the radio support the band received in those cities. Watson appears to suggest that the band might have been even more successful in the States had they been able to tour more widely across the nation in those early years (their touring was structured around their high school holiday periods). Whether that is true, we'll never know. The following chapter does indicate that touring and live shows can be invaluable in enriching a band's image and bank balance.

With that reference to bank balances, let's move on to the issue of sales – and yes, money.

Sales

As *Frogstomp* was climbing the charts, one Sydney newspaper published a shot of Daniel Johns riding his bicycle and the headline: 'How a $6m boy gets to school'. Gillies has dismissed this as merely attention-grabbing, writing: '[The reporter had] clearly just multiplied our album sales at the time – 300,000 – by the album price – $20. If only that were the case' (Gillies et al. 2023: 90).

Gillies has a point. But so, in a way, does that broadsheet.

First, and as stated in the Introduction: *Frogstomp* has been estimated to have sold three million copies globally. This includes an estimated 240,000 copies in Australia during 1995, which is especially impressive given that at that point, 'an album that [sold] 35,000 copies' in that country was 'considered a hit' (Shoebridge 1996). The figure also includes an estimated one million copies sold in the United States.

So, it's an understatement to say that *Frogstomp* was indeed a financial success story. Things get a bit more complicated when we ask whether the three band members enjoyed equal economic rewards. The answer seems to be 'no'. An article published in the *Australian Financial Review* in April 1996 states:

> Songwriting royalties are a key revenue source for many musicians. Songwriters strike deals with music publishing companies, which license songs to record companies, radio stations, TV and movie producers, ad agencies, and so on. Publishers collect fees and royalties and keep 20-40% of the revenue. A 1990 agreement between record companies and music publishers set a royalty rate of 10.6% of the wholesale price of an album. (Shoebridge 1996)

That article reports that 'the songwriting royalties from sales of *Frogstomp* in Australia alone [were] an estimated $508,800' (Shoebridge 1996). The article also acknowledges: 'Four of the 11 songs on *Frogstomp* were written by Johns; the other seven are by Johns and Gillies' (Shoebridge 1996).

So, it appears likely that Johns would have earned – if not $6 million – then at least more than his bandmates. There was reportedly little friction regarding this at the time, though Gillies' father reportedly argued that the royalties should be divided equally among the band members (Gillies et al. 2023: 96). The band eventually came to 'an arrangement where Dan would give a small percentage of his publishing royalties, to me and Chris, and I'd do the same to him and Chris for the songs I wrote' (Gillies et al. 2023: 96). It's unclear whether this arrangement continued beyond *Frogstomp*.

Years later, Gillies would suggest that the royalty division was unfair, writing that 'without the band, the songs may not have been created – that is, the way a band interprets and plays a song can make it even better, and that means the song can reach an audience it might not otherwise have done' (Gillies et al. 2023: 97). He notes: 'There's no right or wrong way to divide royalties, but there is a fair way' (Gillies et al. 2023: 296). Gillies supports this point by citing US legal scholar Sarah Polcz's 2023 study 'Loyalties v. Royalties'. It's useful to briefly examine that study in relation to silverchair's career. Polcz reported that 'groups that split royalties equally among all contributing members, even among members whose contributions are small, produce higher-quality songs, as measured by song revenue and Grammy awards' (2023: 816). *Frogstomp* achieved great success at the ARIA Awards (an Australian equivalent of the Grammys), as Chapter 3 details. Perhaps this success may have been even greater had Gillies and Joannou been more concerned about an equal distribution of royalties. We may never know.[3] 'Quality' is a notoriously subjective assessment. The tracks on the album under discussion are of strong quality, at least in my opinion, and (as Chapter 4 will describe) the band would go on to develop musically in all kinds of exciting ways.

Fans

The band were certainly appreciative of their fan base, which had flourished since the *Nomad* days. This appreciation is best reflected in their fan club, the Llama Appreciation Society. The naming of this club is itself a product of the grunge music era; the boys were inspired by the creature on the front cover of Pearl Jam's album *Vs* (1993), which they believed to be a llama but which turned out to be an angora goat (Gillies et al. 2023: 74)! The llama was, as it happens, an appropriate choice of name; llamas are exotic in Newcastle and across Australia, just as silverchair would become exotic through their international acclaim. The fan club grew with the band's popularity, reaching approximately 7,000 members from Australia, the United States and Europe in August 1999 (Scully 1999).

Membership of Llama included a newsletter entitled 'News from Under the Table', in which the band updated fans on their activities, including latest recordings and forthcoming gigs. In a pre-social media world, newsletters were a popular

---

[3] Polcz also found that 'when participants envisioned the royalty allocation to be with someone with whom they had been friends prior to their creation of a joint work, they exhibited a strong preference for ignoring the difference in contributions and choosing an equal split' (2023: 805). This does not appear to be entirely reflective of silverchair's royalties distribution, at least as Gillies has described this.

way of developing and enhancing parasocial relationships with the folk who bought their music. Parasocial relationships encompass those feelings of connection one has for a public figure – be it a band, singer, TikTok personality or all the above; the feeling that you know and might even be friends with that figure, even if you might never have met and they may have no idea of your existence (Giles 2023). The 'under the table' newsletters were frequently accompanied by small gifts (fridge magnets, stickers), which doubtless contributed to the intimacy.

Yet, while silverchair might have appreciated their fans, there is no denying that some of the band's brushes with the public were awkward. For example, in October 1994, *Beat* (a free-of-charge, street-based Melbourne music newspaper) published a letter from a woman claiming that she had invited silverchair back to her abode and 'took something away from these innocent boys that they'll never be able to give any other girl' (cited in Gillies et al. 2023: 103). The band dismissed this correspondence as 'crap' and indeed the allegations have never been verified (cited in Gillies et al. 2023: 103).

Whether fact or fiction, and even regardless of whether the author was an actual fan, that letter does suggest that silverchair's celebrity was on the rise. After all, which rock star hasn't been the subject of salacious gossip? More seriously, the letter provided a taste of how some members of the public would willingly transgress personal and even physical boundaries to get close to the group.

To expand, there were fans who would make direct contact with band members. Gillies recalls fans parking outside his family home and receiving calls on his home phone from 'screaming teenage girls' (Gillies et al. 2023: 93). If the latter is true, then it suggests silverchair had appeal among the demographic they were ostensibly trying to distance themselves from. The band members and their families also dealt with unsolicited phone calls. Gillies remembers: 'My mum barked down the phone. Chris' grandfather had a chat' (Gillies et al. 2023: 94). Such domestic disturbances were not unprecedented in Australian music history. Some decades earlier, fans regularly encroached upon the Sydney home of George Young and Stevie Wright when they were members of the pop group The Easybeats. The address had been published by a magazine. Young recalled that while being a pop star was great for meeting girls, he was not fond of discovering them hiding in the wardrobe and under the bed, saying: 'My parents are furious' (cited in Apter 2020). The silverchair boys and their families appear to have experienced a similar sense of mortification when their own private spaces were invaded.

The trio dealt with their newfound notoriety in different ways. Johns told one reporter that he remained grounded by 'staying in school . . . cos if you get a big head in school, you get [made fun of] a lot' (cited in Much Music 1995). The reality was more complicated. Gillies would recall: 'For the most part, Chris and I laughed things off', whereas Johns 'went between liking the attention and loathing it' (Gillies et al. 2023: 94). These differences may reflect the different kinds of contact they had with fans. Gillies remembers: 'People came up to me and Chris wanting to crack jokes . . . whereas people came up to Dan carrying 200-page diaries detailing their various acts of self-harm' (Gillies et al. 2023: 94). John Watson recalls:

A number of the more obsessive crazies that would come after Daniel seemed to be women about his mother's age who had often had . . . terminations around the time that Daniel had been born, and they became obsessed with this idea that Daniel was the son that they had never had. There were many of these people. There was one in particular who was French, who used to send these long missives, and she kept turning up at gigs in Europe. And like, she was recognised by face. (Johns 2021: Episode 1)

Gillies further acknowledges that Johns received a majority of the media attention, being the frontman. The widely circulated paparazzi shots of the singer riding his bicycle to school – a remarkably mundane act, one that many young Australians engage in every day – signalled to him and others that privacy was something he had lost.

Given the above, it is easy to speculate that the overnight fame and the emotional intensity of certain fans have at least contributed to Johns' own challenges. In the years following *Frogstomp*, he waged highly publicized battles with anxiety, anorexia nervosa and substance abuse. These conditions are complex and cannot be attributed to a single cause; none of them are restricted to folk in the public eye. I think it's fair to say that shifting so rapidly from anonymous schoolboy to global star who was followed by the press and obsessive listeners could not have helped.[4]

____

[4] The book *Can Music Make You Sick?* (2020) provides a comprehensive overview of the multifaceted relationship between music-making and poor health.

'chair parents

I want here to look briefly at the parents of the silverchair members and the practical and emotional support that they provided during those early years. It'd be an understatement to say that without this support, the band would never have reached the heights they did.

As mentioned, all three families lived in working-class Newcastle. The parents were, it seems, completely unfamiliar with the music industry prior to *Nomad*, being employed in 'blue collar' jobs (Gillies et al. 2023: 10). Gillies' father was a plumber, Johns' father worked at the Newcastle fruit markets and Joannou's mother was employed at a dry-cleaners. The very fact that they allowed their offspring to pursue music careers is thus a testament to the trust and belief that they held in silverchair. Gillies claims that his father introduced him to Led Zeppelin, which 'put me on my musical path' (Gillies et al. 2023: 37). Gillies specifically remembers Zeppelin's song 'Nobody's Fault but Mine' (1976) as being the track that turned him onto the British rockers.

In 2023, Gillies recalled that the parents 'helped to create the merch – t-shirts, hoodies, tote bags and the like – and sold them at gigs and through the fan club' (Gillies et al. 2023: 82). The parents were responsible for driving their kids to gigs and for writing, photocopying and posting off copies of the band's newsletter. This labour was performed on top of the parents' own day jobs. Gillies does not explain why the record label did not produce the newsletter, only that the parents were enthusiastic to do so, especially when they – like their offspring – started to reap financial rewards.

The 'chair parents would also be important sources of advice and encouragement for the band. Joannou recalls his mother talking him out of quitting the band's first European tour. She reportedly told her son: 'You can't let your friends down, Chris. . . . Let's just get through this leg of the tour and see what happens' (cited in Gillies et al. 2023: 85). Gillies remembers his father telling him: 'You're no better than anyone else. . . . It doesn't matter who you are, how much money you make or how many CDs you sell, you can drop dead as quick as the next guy walking down the street' (cited in Gillies et al. 2023: 93). This kind of advice helped the young man stay grounded as silverchair's fame escalated.

And, the parents sacrificed. They sacrificed their spare time with chauffeuring duties, merch sales and newsletter production. They sacrificed their own privacy as fans phoned and parked outside their houses. And I'm sure they sacrificed many hours of sleep as 1995 wore on.

What was going through the minds of the silverchair mums and dads as their offspring became internationally successful? The parents themselves have provided little media commentary on this or indeed any other topic. The boys have provided some speculation, with Gillies recalling: 'The parents wanted the best for the band' and this is reflected in the work they undertook for silverchair (Gillies et al. 2023: 82). He also describes them as 'protective', though they do not appear to have been unduly so; the boys were, for instance, allowed to record with Kevin Shirley despite the parents noticing the 'gradually emptying bottle of Jack Daniels [sitting] on the desk throughout every session he worked on' (Apter 2018: 40). One can only imagine what was going through the parents' head as band members (namely Johns) injured themselves, and one of their songs was implicated in a real-life murder case.

Reviewing *Frogstomp*

My choice to focus in this section of the chapter on music reviews is deliberate; during the 1990s, these were a key site of public exposure and deliberation for musical acts (Evans 1998). These reviews belonged to the broader pantheon of music journalism, which has historically played a significant role in determining what becomes popular and considered worthy of public discussion:

> Together with other mass media newspapers and magazines, journalists and editors act as gatekeepers, to an extent controlling what becomes popular and what does not. While radio and television programs simply play music (or choose not to), music magazines and music journalists need to justify in words what they let through the gates. Such justification or support can take the form of a simple picture caption endorsing an artist, or be an extended piece of writing based on research and interviews. (Michelsen 2015: 216)

As a teenager, I would routinely read reviews published in *Beat*, *Rolling Stone Australia/NZ* and *Juice* to determine whether I should invest my hard-earned pocket money in a particular CD. Reviews also gave me a sense of what was 'cool' (and therefore worth listening to) and 'uncool' (and therefore to be avoided or at least not admit to listening to). My own musical decisions were further influenced by the recommendations of friends, many of whom were silverchair aficionados and one of whom recorded *Frogstomp* onto cassette tape for my listening pleasure.

Happily, the critics were saying largely (though not exclusively) positive things. *Sydney Morning Herald* journalist Shane Danielsen described *Frogstomp* as 'an impressive debut' (cited in Apter 2018: 44). Writing in Melbourne's *Age* newspaper, David Saunders (1995: 18) praised the album as a 'damn fine recording by a band whose members barely had time to pinch themselves, much less pay their dues in the industry'. Saunders lauded the band's 'lyrical maturity well beyond their years and some tight, interest-sustaining playing' (1995: 18). He wasn't the only reviewer to describe silverchair as possessing an almost preternaturally mature talent. US music critic Jim Testa (1995) wrote: 'That it comes from Australia is surprising enough; that it was produced by three 15-year-olds is nothing short of amazing.' Ron Givens was less charitable, writing in the US magazine *Stereo Review* that the album had 'potential' but that silverchair had some growing up to do: 'If these guys did a little more living and a little less listening (to other bands' records), they could make something cool' (1996: 142).

There were inevitable comparisons with Seattle rock. Sometimes, these were unfavourable. For example, US music journalist Robert Christgau wrote that silverchair sounds 'exactly like Pearl Jam except no good' (1995: 52). Other critics were less dismissive. Testa described 'Cicada' as silverchair's answer to Pearl Jam's 1992 track 'Jeremy'. This track was based on a real-life case of a young boy who died by suicide in the classroom where he endured vicious bullying. *Rolling Stone*'s David Fricke (1995) wrote that '[too] much has been made of . . . the Aussie trio's superficial resemblances to Pearl Jam and Soundgarden'. For Fricke, a lack of originality was hardly uncommon nor a crime for a teenage band, adding: 'Truly shameless [grunge] wanna-be's [sic] like Bush should be so lucky to have the hard smarts that' silverchair demonstrate. Bush was the British grunge band whose lead singer Gavin Rossdale's vocals bore an uncanny resemblance to Kurt Cobain's.

The concept of generations is explicitly invoked by a review published in the South Australian newspaper *Port Lincoln Times*. The reviewer, Clayton Bester, wrote: 'My overall impression of this album is one of despair which is a little worrying if the next generation feels we will leave them with a world full of doom, and gloom' (1995: 35). The 'we' presumably refers to Baby Boomers or at least those older than the 'chair guys. Bester is quick to point out that he is not criticizing the band, noting: 'To the younger generation this is an album full of music which really kicks and should be treated as such' (1995: 35).

Some reviewers discussed the actual lyrical content. Bester (1995) reads 'Israel's Son' as chronicling 'alienation, loneliness and intense hatred of being left out to the point of killing'. For Bester (1995), the fact that silverchair addressed such 'heavy topics' was 'a sign of real song-writing talent'. *Los Angeles Times* reviewer Lorraine Ali praises Johns and Gillies for having 'mastered the art of writing a good song' (1995: 1). Ali described the songs as being 'like teen anthems, as catchy and rebellious as Cheap Trick's "Surrender" days, but as sonically booming as new bands like Helmet (minus the intensity)' (1995: 1)

These reviews are significant inasmuch as they signal the enthusiasm that *Frogstomp*'s initial critics felt for the band.

For all the Seattle comparisons, there were folk who were willing to look deeper and acknowledge the band's talent and potential. Yet even many of the positive *Frogstomp* reviews were not quite able to think of silverchair outside of references to youthfulness or Seattle grunge. Fricke (1995) actually closed his brief review by writing: 'When these guys turn 18, they'll be really dangerous.' The suggestion here is that only adulthood would strip the band of their novelty status and allow them to become serious musicians.

3   silverchair live

This chapter examines three of silverchair's live appearances during 1994–5. Two of these – the Big Day Out 1995 shows and the performance that was recorded for the Australian music video of 'Pure Massacre' – help reinforce the band's image as grunge kings of the mosh pit. The band's (non-)appearances at the 1995 ARIA Awards were criticized as immature and insensitive towards fans; I argue that they actually showcase a heretofore unremarked humour. All three performances are ripe for analysis because they demonstrate how silverchair sought to construct a sense of imagined community among their fans and with other alternative Australian acts. The concept of 'imagined communities' has been borrowed from political scientist Benedict Anderson (1983), who used it to describe the ways in which individuals who would likely have no personal knowledge of one another become unified, even if only in a virtual sense, by their consumption of printed texts. This concept can be extended to the use of other media.

Playing live

The term 'live music' applies to music performances that take place in real time and outside studio settings (Auslander 2023; Brown and Knox 2017; Frith 2007, 2010). In the 2020s, this can involve holograms of acts that have disbanded[1] or where artists are deceased and musos performing on a livestream from their lounge rooms (this was popular during the early Covid years). This chapter will focus on the more traditional modes of live music, whereby flesh-and-blood performers play music on a stage watched by audiences while situated within the same venue.

There are several key features of live music that I wish to discuss here, because they are relevant to the case studies below. Perhaps most importantly, live performances have commonly been understood as bastions of authenticity, or at least promising something authentic, with this authenticity commonly understood as resulting from the merging of the aural and the visual. Auslander (2023: 97) describes one perception that I have myself heard expressed in conversations with friends and strangers about live gigs:

> Recorded sound is perceived as insufficient to provide a complete experience of music. As has been amply demonstrated both theoretically and empirically, the visual information provided by musicians in performance shapes the listener's perception and experience of the music, not only in indicating emphasis and expressing emotion, but also in conveying such basic structural features as rhythm and pitch.

---

[1] One example would be ABBA Voyage, a concert tour in which the 1970s supergroup (whose members are indeed still alive!) appears in holographic form.

In live shows, this visual element can be captured; the audience can see the artist's body language and hear their tone of voice. The artist can provide commentary about the songs rather than simply playing them.

In the realm of Oz Rock, I suggest that the enduring appeal of live music may relate to the specific brand of Australian masculinity that this genre connotes. Shane Homan writes that in Oz Rock mythology, performing in pubs has often been seen as an apprenticeship for up-and-coming bands (Homan 2003: 167). This was an apprenticeship that the silverchair boys undertook, playing at several licenced venues during their early years while still being too young to buy a beer. Significantly, pubs have historically been highly masculinized domains, characterized by drunken and uncouth behaviour among patrons, as well as hostility towards groups coded as 'other' (women, gays) (Hawkins 2014: 87; Oldham 2013: 121). So, we can assume that this apprenticeship pertains not only to musical skills; it's also an apprenticeship in impressing the denizens of blokey venues.

Finally, live performances, and especially touring, can have financial benefits for artists. This has particularly been so since the rise of music streaming and downloading during the 2000s and the corresponding drop in album sales. Yet even in 1995, it was clear that touring could fatten an act's bank balance. For example, *Frogstomp* sales in America jumped considerably following the band's first tour; Johns' biographer Jeff Apter notes that by the time of silverchair's Chicago concert, the album 'had sold 5000 copies, 2000 in Atlanta alone, where it debuted at number eleven . . . before it was fully stocked in stores. The following week, sales doubled' (2018: 51).

Audiences for live music

A growing body of research has developed around the experiences of audiences for live music (Brown and Knox 2017; Tsioulakis and Hytönen-Ng 2016). Among other questions, this research has asked: What are the factors that attract us to watch our favourite acts in stadiums, pubs and, increasingly, online? The answers proffered below are not the only ones; they are the ones most relevant to the readings of the three silverchair performances.

First, live performances can enhance the likelihood that fan and idol might meet. This was particularly the case in the years before social media 'liking' and 'sharing', when 'your best chance of reciprocal interaction with a media figure was a chance meeting in physical space' (Giles 2023: 34). These interactions are usually one-sided. To elaborate, the fan can see the performer even if they are just a dot on the horizon; they can call out well wishes, profess their love – but there's no guarantee the performer can see or hear the fan. Nonetheless, the prospect that one's idol might see or hear is always present, and maybe, just maybe, you might actually come into contact with that singer or bassist or drummer (Brown and Knox 2017: 238).

Second, attending live performances can mean bearing witness to a particular moment of an act's career. This was reported by participants in Brown and Knox's 2017 study of live music audiences. Sometimes, audiences consciously attend a concert because they feel they will not get another opportunity to see that act live; farewell tours or 'one-off reunion shows' are good examples of this (Brown and Knox

2017: 242). On other occasions, it would become clear only in retrospect that a live show represented a specific 'chapter' in that act's timeline (Brown and Knox 2017: 242). The audiences for the performances described below may well have attended to hear *Frogstomp* songs; they may have had a sensational time. It's unclear whether any were thinking at the moment that they were witnessing the band's '*Frogstomp* era' or their 'grunge era'.

Finally, live performances can create a sense of imagined community among attendees. Anderson argued that the nation 'is imagined as community because, regardless of the actual inequality and exploitation that may prevail in each, the nation is always conceived as a deep, horizontal comradeship' (1983: 7). This concept can be useful in helping us to understand the particular thrill for audiences of attending live music gigs. To illustrate, at these gigs, attendees are joined together, if only fleetingly, to communally celebrate a music act they all enjoy. This can take the form of singing along, whistling, applauding, writhing in the mosh pit or wearing merchandise associated with an act or music scene.

Of course, the imagined community does not suddenly evaporate when the performance finishes; it continues as the fans listen to their idol's music on Spotify, like their updates on Instagram and read about them in magazines (Hill 2014: 182). Nonetheless, there is something especially intimate and, indeed, unique about physically gathering with other fans. One study actually describes the live concert thus: 'An unrepeatable, exclusive event, grounded in time and space, envelops fan identity, of which performers on stage are a part' (Bennett 2015: 14).

silverchair were highly attuned to this community-building, both within their audiences and within the wider network of Australian alternative musicians. This will become evident in the three performances discussed below.

silverchair as a live band

Devoting an entire chapter to silverchair's live performances was a no-brainer, given that the band prided themselves on being a premium live act. Gillies recalls that during their early years, '[o]ur focus was on playing live shows because that's what we loved. A happy by-product of doing so many shows was that people realised we were a real band who could actually play' (Gillies et al. 2023: 80). Review after review cited the passion of their shows. For example, the *Chicago Tribune* wrote that 'there was no denying the savvy sense of dynamics, muscular melodies and tight ensemble playing . . . Silverchair has the potential to match the impact of some of its influences' – with those influences including Black Sabbath and Deep Purple (Kot 1995: 12). Reviewing a gig at popular West Hollywood venue The Whisky a Go Go, the *Los Angeles Times* reported that the group 'launched into its songs with such power and focus that it put vaguely similar bands like Catherine Wheel,[2] which has at least 10 years life experience on it, to shame' (Ali 1995: 1).

____

[2]Catharine Wheel were a British alternative rock band who were active during the 1990s.

silverchair were a particularly busy live act during 1995, performing gigs in Australia, the United States, Canada and Britain (Silverchair Concert History). This was itself unique given that the members were still teenagers and their trips had to be negotiated with their high school (where they would remain until graduating in 1997). This was an obstacle that musicians even a few years older did not face. John O'Donnell would describe the restricted opportunity to tour as being 'a blessing and a curse. . . . At times we wished we could have exposed them more, but their limited availability probably fuelled demand and added to the mystique surrounding the group' (cited in Shoebridge 1996).

International touring was an especially big deal for a band whose members had been novices to travelling. Prior to jetting out of Australia, Joannou recalls telling a reporter: 'Is it my first time to Europe? It's my first trip out of Newy!' (Gillies et al. 2023: 85). This statement might have been made in jest, but it also points to the modest, working-class nature of the band members' lives up until that point. The very fact that they were chosen to perform as pre-show entertainment at the 1995 MTV Music Awards in September that year is testament to their meteoric global rise. The band thrashed out 'Tomorrow' and 'Pure Massacre' on the roof of Radio City Hall while guests strutted down the red carpet below.

The performances discussed below have been chosen because they each provide insightful examples of the band constructing and – in one case, poking fun at – their grunge god personas, evoking the authenticity that was such a defining feature of grunge and alternative music and building a sense of community among fans and other alternative

Australian acts. None of these performances took place as part of an actual tour, and all took place in Australia.

I should clarify that I attended none of the three gigs described below. My discussions of each emerge from (re-)watching recordings and reading media reports almost thirty years after they were held and over a decade after silverchair disbanded. I am therefore unable to comment on the unique *experience* of each gig – the sights, the smells, the warm glow of communal fan worship.

The Australian 'Pure Massacre' video

The 'Pure Massacre' video is an appropriate case study because of its reliance on notions of live-ness and authenticity to promote the song, album and band. The video was shot in December 1994 at the Phoenician Club, a popular music venue in Sydney's inner city that had previously played host to Nirvana (Gillies et al. 2023: 71). The clip was directed by Robert Hambling, who had previously directed the band's 'Tomorrow' clip, and was released in Australia in January 1995.

The clip opens with a close-up of a hand striking a match, followed by a close-up of the band playing their instruments. Is this studio footage? That question is scotched in spectacular fashion when the clip cuts to an audience rocking out to their idols playing on stage. The cut comes at the 0.39-second mark, just as the guitars fire up. We've been transported to an actual silverchair gig; the flame has morphed into an explosion of energy.

In the following four minutes, there is a strong emphasis on the excitement of attendees. For instance, there are multiple shots of moshing, which had by the mid-1990s become a signature practice at grunge and other alternative rock gigs. Moshing is where concertgoers 'hurl their bodies at one another in a dance area called a "pit"' (Tsitsos 1999: 397). This 'pit is not an explicitly marked off area, but … usually form[s] in front of the stage where a band is playing' (Tsitsos 1999: 405). Sometimes, there can be several pits in one venue. Moshing is foremost a mode of aggressive dancing, a corporeal response to the hard rock being played. William Tsitsos (1999) suggests that moshing might also be read as a form of rebellion against a ubiquitous, implicitly docile mainstream. With this in mind, it's perhaps unsurprising that very early examples of this practice could be witnessed at UK punk shows during the 1970s (Ragusa 2021). An early manifestation was pogoing, a dance style that was popularized by Sex Pistols performer Sid Vicious and that involved 'the crowd jumping up and down, arms tightly against their sides, almost like a box of pens being shaken' (Ragusa 2021).

Throughout 'Pure Massacre', there are also shots of stage-diving patrons. Stage diving involves someone – either an attendee or indeed the artist whose show it is – jumping into the audience during a performance. Like moshing, stage diving appears to have had its genesis during the 1970s, with Iggy Pop being an early exponent (Ihaza 2017). Joannou recalled that stage diving was emphasized in the video because 'that was so much a part of the grunge scene at the time' (Gillies et al. 2023: 71). He claims that stage diving was meant to be shot during their pre-show sound check and interspersed with footage of the concert. What transpired was quite different:

> When we hit the stage for real later in the night, the sea of sweaty kids went ballistic. No one could stop the stage-diving that was to come. It was inevitable . . . Robert filmed the whole thing, and got some epic shots of people – many of them screaming girls – launching themselves through the air . . . Robert also filmed the doors left of stage heaving back and forth as the chains and padlock holding them closed were being stretched by people pushing against them trying to get into the gig. (Gillies et al. 2023: 72)

This passage reads like self-mythologizing on Joannou's part, and it sidesteps the very real harms that such behaviour can cause. This is harm that silverchair would become intimately familiar with. At a Melbourne gig in November 1995, Johns stage-dived into the audience, only for nobody to catch him. The injured singer was rushed to hospital, where fortunately his recovery was swift (MTV News 1995). Two months earlier, at a show at Santa Monica Pier, Johns had been hit on the eye by a full beer bottle propelled from the crowd. He finished the tune, bloodied and bruised, before being transported to hospital.

Nonetheless, Joannou's reminiscence does remind us that the video derives its key frisson from the sense of being propelled into an actual concert. The various elements – banging door, crowd surfing, bodies bashing against each other – accelerate the song's pulsing intensity and reinforce a popular image of what a live grunge show – and specifically, a silverchair concert – should look like. This is the authentic experience of watching a band that prided themselves on being authentic, the real deal, not hostages to commercial demands.

The timing of the 'Pure Massacre' video is absolutely crucial in appreciating the visual punch it still packs. When the video was shot, silverchair had been famous in Australia for only a few months. Their debut album had not even been released. It's a testament, then, to their talent and their onstage dynamic that they could incite a crowd to respond with such animalistic fervour.

Let's now compare the Australian music video for 'Pure Massacre' with the one recorded for a North American audience and directed by English musician and director Peter Christopherson. Christopherson was an appropriate choice; he founded the independent band Throbbing Gristle, which 'dealt in unsettling grey noise underpinned with clanking electronic rhythms and lyrics betraying a fascination with serial killers, fascism, sadism and death' (Petridis 2010). Themes such as these appear on the *Frogstomp* album and, indeed, in the song under discussion.

The Christopherson version of 'Pure Massacre' was one of three reshot for that audience. The others were 'Tomorrow' and 'Israel's Son', with those US videos being directed by different directors.[3] The US 'Pure Massacre' clip opens with a shot of a dog trotting across an industrial landscape. The video cuts to the band performing in an underground bunker. Further shots of the canine are interspersed with blurred shots of faceless figures pounding the ground violently with sharp tools,

---

[3] The US 'Tomorrow' video was directed by Mark Pellington, while the US 'Israel's Son' video was directed by Nigel Dick.

perhaps scythes. Are they manual labourers, murderers or both? These are followed by scenes of young people slipping into the bunker to watch the band.

Strikingly, the two videos present very different interpretations of the song. The Australian clip evokes not just a sense of liveness but also a sense of celebration and unity. The crowd becomes a kind of community, revelling in the shared experience of moshing out to their idols. The video is shot almost entirely in black and white, giving it a gritty, documentary aesthetic, and positioning the viewer as a fly on the wall, watching but not quite able to join in the festivities.

Conversely, the US clip evokes the nightmarish, disorienting mise-en-scène of the lyrics. The video jumps between black-and-white and colour cinematography, while the visuals become blurred at different points. Though it's not all grimness. Attractive youngsters stumble into view and quickly become entranced by the rockers they've encountered. These shots can be read as a metaphor for both the American discovery of silverchair and, generally, for the vision of the world upheld by the song – and indeed upheld by grunge music as a genre.

Big Day Out 1995

Among silverchair's best-known earliest live performances are those undertaken as part of the Big Day Out (BDO) festival in January–February 1995. It's worth revisiting this performance because of its prominent role in both 1990s alternative Australian music culture and in the band's growing popularity.

First, some h story: the BDO began in 1992 and encompassed a one-day music festival. This festival initially took place in Sydney only; in the following years, it moved around the country to Melbourne, Perth, Gold Coast and Adelaide, as well as Auckland in New Zealand. The BDO showcased Austra ian and international acts that might be regarded as alternative or indie/independent (Jones 2015: 31). The first BDO hosted Nirvana, who had recently achieved global success on the back of their single 'Smells Like Teen Spirit' and album *Nevermind* (1991). In 1995, silverchair played alongside the likes of Hole, The Offspring, Kim Salmon (who, as we saw in Chapter 1, credits himself with an early Antipodean use of the word 'grunge') and Aboriginal rock/country group Warumpi Band. The bands played on stages dotted around an assigned open-air venue.

Importantly, BDO's alternative/indie credentials extend to more than the acts playing. Attendees frequently embraced an alternative/subcultural aesthetic. A 2015 study recalls that this 'festival became a pilgrimage for fans, who donned their "festival attire" – namely a band t-shirt, some cut-off army pants, a pair of Chucks/Doc Martens, colored hair, and DIY attitudes – and jo ned fellow lovers of rock music to show allegiance to their favorite bands and perform their fandom' (Jones 2015: 32). The wearing of this attire helped create a sense of community, one based around alternative music and an implicit opposition to the mainstream.

Interestingly, the BDO took place in January and February – summe months in the Southern Hemisphere. The festival coincided with the triple j Hottest 100, which gave the impression (to me, anyway!) of there being one giant, sun-drenched celebration of alternative music. It should be acknowledged, though, that there is no evidence that these two musical events were in any way connected.

In the pre-social media era, festivals such as BDO were a pivotal mode of promotion for emerging acts. Adelle Robinson, the current chair of the Australian Festival Association, explains:

> Festival shows … are a very important part of the artist life cycle. A festival is where breakthrough acts can prove themselves to new audiences. The format of a festival means exposure to larger audiences outside of an artist's core market. It is a place to discover new music. (cited in Quinn 2024)

The 1995 BDO offered a significant early promotion for silverchair, coming as it did in the period between the release of 'Tomorrow' and *Frogstomp*. The festival contributed to the band's growing public profile and quite possibly attracted new fans.

Happily, evidence suggests that BDO audiences liked what they saw of the Newcastle rockers. *Rolling Stone* reported that silverchair's Sydney performance drew a crowd of '15,000 people – three times the regular capacity of the stage area' the band performed on, while at the Melbourne show 'kids were actually diving off nearby rooftops into the audience and trampolining on the protective canvas hanging over the band' (Fricke 1996). Nick Launay, an esteemed British music producer who had produced albums by high-profile groups such as Midnight Oil and The Birthday Party and who would later collaborate with the 'chair, remembers:

> There were more people interested in seeing them at age fourteen than all those big bands, and they couldn't fit enough

people. And so people were climbing on roofs, they were climbing up lamp posts. It was absolutely amazing. It was like footage I've seen of The Beatles. It was just teenagers losing it and grown-ups, too. (Johns 2021: Episode 1)

Put simply, the kind of crowd enthusiasm depicted in the Australian 'Pure Massacre' video was playing out yet again. The punters were not the only ones who found the BDO shows memorable. In 2023, Chris Joannou wrote that these performances were 'how I like to remember Silverchair . . . in our element, on stage, playing loud, and letting loose' (Gillies et al. 2023: 332).

Though, of course, all good things must eventually end, and both silverchair and the BDO are no exceptions. The BDO toured for the final time in 2014, only three years after the Newcastle boys called it a day. Jones writes that the festival 'had become both too expensive and too eclectic' (2015: 36). The line-up had adopted the random, multi-genre format of a digital music app, and that was not necessarily a good thing.

What made the BDO work were the links to the indie music scene and the performance, as well as the embodiment of this fandom in a communal space.

While technology is great for individual customisation of musical playlists, a festival needs that thread of community and like-mindedness to maintain its identity. Without it the scene is void of meaning and authenticity. (Jones 2015: 36)

By 2014, then, the BDO and silverchair represented not only alternative Australian music but also a moment in alternative

Australian music history that had been consigned to memories. And fond memories, at that.

The 1995 ARIA Music Awards

Since their inception in 1987, the ARIA Music Awards (hereafter 'the ARIAs') ceremony has been a major event in Australia's popular music calendar. Like most awards ceremonies, the ARIAs play an important role in 'validat(ing) forms of culture, giving a status to the successful artist and setting a pattern for cultural judgement within their field' (Street 2014: 182). The ceremony is televised and receives considerable media coverage, thereby promoting the work of awardees and nominees.

The 1995 ARIAs was held at the Sydney Convention and Exhibition Centre on 2 October 1995. This show marked a high point in silverchair's early success, providing further evidence that they were becoming a force to be reckoned with in the Australian music industry. The band won five awards that evening: three for 'Tomorrow' – Single of the Year, Highest Selling Single, Breakthrough Artist-Single – as well as Breakthrough Artist-Album (*Frogstomp*) and Best New Talent.

The 1995 ARIAs were also significant inasmuch as the awards were framed in distinctly generational terms. Host Richard Stubbs (a high-profile Australian radio presenter and comedian) opened proceedings by remarking: 'This past year or so has seen a changing of the guard in Australian music. A whole generation of fabulous new acts have leapt up and grabbed the industry by the throat.'[4] Stubbs was not the only person making such statements around that time. In a 30 September issue of *Billboard* magazine, Christie Eliezer wrote that '1995 was the year when – led by the phenomenal success of teenage grunge act silverchair . . . that the new guard took charge' of the Australian music industry (1995: 65).

The generationalism suggested above is invoked and contested in two of the best-remembered silverchair appearances from that evening. The first of these is the combined awarding of the Best New Talent, Debut Single and Debut Album. These gongs were all accepted by Kevin Shirley's seven-year-old son, Josh. The band's Best Single award was accepted by Shirley himself. The band's absence ruffled a few feathers. One reporter wrote that the band 'dudded the public and the press' (Holmes 1995: 127). Another reporter called it 'insulting and self-righteous', a 'slap in the face' to the Australian music industry (Te Koha 1995b: 13). Popular Australian music commentator Molly Meldrum was allegedly 'disappointed' but suggested that silverchair's actions were largely driven by the fact that they were 'very media shy' (cited in Te Koha 1995a: 11).

If these kinds of responses sound familiar, then they should. Mark Davis (1997) has demonstrated how 1990s Australian media was quick to castigate young people for all manner of poor behaviour. GenX, he writes, were 'caught on the wrong side of an increasing gap between official sanctioned culture and renegade culture' (1997: viii). In commentaries such as those described above, silverchair are stereotyped as

---

[4] This 'new generation' included fellow ARIA nominees such as You Am I, Merril Bainbridge, Max Sharam and Christine Anu.

renegades; they are accused of disappointing their audiences because they refused to do the bare minimum and accept their awards.

For their part, silverchair have suggested that their non-appearances were part of a gag gone wrong. Gillies and Joannou explained in 2023 that they 'thought it would be funnier to send up the only other person who played on *Frogstomp*' – their producer's son – and that 'this connection was meant to be explained by the presenter, who was Meatloaf' (Gillies et al. 2023: 43). The 'Bat Out of Hell' singer presented the Best New Talent, Debut Single and Debut Album trio of awards; evidently, he wasn't reading the autocue. Interestingly, no excuses have been provided by the presenters of the other two awards; perhaps their attention to detail failed them, too.

The lack of clarity regarding the reasons for silverchair's non-appearances at the 1995 ARIAs has left them open to multiple readings. I do not claim that the readings I will now proffer somehow capture 'the truth' of what happened, just that they make the band's contributions to the awards ceremony all the more interesting.

First, the non-appearances can be read as a sort of anti-establishment posturing, with the 'establishment' here represented by the ARIAs. This reading might seem glib, but it's worth remembering other instances of acting up at award shows. At the same ARIAs ceremony, Paul Mac (who would later collaborate with Daniel Johns) thanked 'Sydney's ecstasy dealers' when his group Itch-E and Scratch-E won Best Dance Release (cited in Fox and Doyle 2018). This generated a minor controversy; playful references to illicit substances had seldom been heard at such a mainstream, televised event.

Earlier, in 1981, the iconic Oz Rock band Cold Chisel famously acted up at the TV Week/Countdown[5] Music Awards. The band was nominated for seven of the major awards at that ceremony and won them all. They did not appear on stage to accept the accolades, though they did close the ceremony by performing their song 'My Turn to Cry'. This rendition included 're-written verses' which 'damned the awards and savaged *TV Week* for its superficial support of the music industry and its sudden embracing of the band' (O'Donnell 1991). The group then destroyed their instruments and the set before leaving the stage. This appearance definitely anticipates the content of silverchair's 1995 ARIA (non-)appearances, though it's unclear whether the Newcastle boys were inspired by that earlier episode.

Second, the (non-)appearances can be read as a kind of riposte to those who had dismissed the band as an infantile Nirvana clone. silverchair ended up winning prestigious awards, and these were collected by an *actual* child who, with his long golden hair and flannelette jacket, resembled a younger Daniel Johns. There is certainly an amusing petulance to the band's refusal to accept their gongs. It's almost as though they were saying: 'You said we were annoying little brats, now we're gonna prove it!'

A striking aspect of that latter reading is that it highlights silverchair's humorous side. They may have hit the big-time singing about carnage and misery, but they also had a flair

---

5 *TV Week* is a long-running television and pop culture-oriented Australian magazine. *Countdown* was a popular music-focused television program that ran from 1974 to 1987. The music awards ceremony mentioned above was a joint project between these two entities.

for comedy. This comedy was elsewhere jet black, as might befit a grunge band. For instance, during their Santa Monica show, the month before the ARIAs, Johns introduced 'Faultline' by declaring: 'The next song is about premature babies and ejaculation' (Laj 1995). Several years later, Johns would introduce their 1997 track 'Cemetery' as being about a 'male prostitute' (cited in Apter 2018: 96).

Further, the non-appearances can also be read as an expression of the band's opposition to fame and celebrity. They achieved this by removing as much of themselves – and particularly, as much of their reputations as Seattle rock clones – as possible. First, they did not collect their awards. When the band at last materialized on stage, in the final moments, it was to perform a cover version of Radio Birdman's 'New Race' (1977). Formed during the 1970s and based in Australia, Radio Birdman were influenced by non-mainstream US bands such as MC5 and The Stooges. The band's name was taken from a misheard lyric in The Stooges' song '1970' (Stafford 2024). By covering this classic track, silverchair were signalling their participation in an imagined transnational community of alternative music. This sense of community was further emphasized by their invitation to Tim Rogers to join them in the number. Rogers' band You Am I had just won the Best Alternative Album award for their sophomore record *Hi-Fi Way*; silverchair had cited that group as an inspiration.

The actual choice of song is itself another example of the band's wit. It's not difficult to read the choice of 'New Race' as a humorous acknowledgement that 'kids' – the silverchair trio and Tim Rogers (whose band formed in 1989) – are going to defeat that pesky old guard, albeit metaphorically. They're not content to be dismissed as Antipodean Nirvana wannabes. The question of generations is also pertinent here. This is a song about young people, remember. The 'New Race' that Radio Birdman were singing about back in 1977 were the young folk of the 1970s; the song was a 'tongue in cheek response' to their manager's, Charles Fisher, request for them to write a 'teen anthem' (Deniztek undated). It's easy to read the 'kids' in the ARIAs cover as being the young people of the 1990s, whose angst silverchair and Rogers were supposedly channelling.

I want to close this chapter by comparing the 'New Race' number with the band's performance at the MTV Music Awards. The performances happened within a month of each other, and yet, visually, there is a notable difference. At the MTV Awards, silverchair were positioned outside, playing as A-listers streamed into the venue at the start. Conversely, in 'New Race', the boys are well and truly inside the building. Their absences throughout the ceremony make their materialization all the more remarkable. By playing at the end, they are effectively having the final word of the night.

4 The years after 'Tomorrow'

This chapter explores silverchair's movements in the years following *Frogstomp*. The chapter opens with a survey of each subsequent album. The purpose is to chart the group's profound musical development. We examine the circumstances surrounding the band's widely publicized demise and the animosity that currently exists between members. The chapter looks at how silverchair's influence lives on in a selection of current Australian acts. We then return to the 1995 record to investigate the various ways in which *Frogstomp* is remembered by band members and music critics. These acts of remembering are situated within the context of Web 2.0, where fans have the capacity to share and bond over content regarding their idols, and a broader 1990s nostalgia.

Subsequent albums

My readings of each post-*Frogstomp* album take into account my impression of that work and a snapshot of its production and critical reception. These readings are not as comprehensive as the one provided for *Frogstomp* in Chapter 2, but they will help give the reader a sense of the band's growth beyond 1995.

The sophomore album *Freak Show* was released in Australia by Murmur in January 1997. The lead single, 'Freak', gave listeners an idea of what was in store this time around. Amidst a backdrop of grinding guitars and thrashing drums, Johns howls about how the song's title applies to him. There's a recurring theme of poor self-image, which is also invoked in 'Abuse Me' and 'Pop Song for Us Rejects'. This theme was popular in 1990s rock, grunge and otherwise; think about Nirvana's 'Pennyroyal Tea' (1993) or Radiohead's 'Creep' (1993). Grim imagery, especially intimations of hatred, animates a majority of the tracks on this record.

Yet, while silverchair had strayed not far from their first album thematically, it was a slightly different story musically. Track 6, 'Cemetery', which was also the album's third single, features a string section and a tenderness in Johns' singing that had seldom been heard previously. He does a 360 on Track 9, 'Learn to Hate', where his piercing vocals are more redolent of heavy metal than Seattle grunge. The soft-loud shift that characterized *Frogstomp* tracks appears sparingly; 'Abuse Me', the second single, offers one example.

The *Los Angeles Times* called the album 'a powerful and gloriously imperfect work of sludgy, scrappy garage metal' (Scribner 1997). This sums up *Freak Show* nicely.

Aesthetically, too, the band had commenced their move away from the mosh pit. Joannou and Gillies would shave their heads. Johns would sport dreadlocks and an eyebrow ring. They looked 'alternative', yes, but this was a different kind of alternative to their 1995 deportment.

The band's third album, *Neon Ballroom* (1999), represented silverchair's first truly dramatic change in pace. Okay, there are angsty lyrics. There are heavy rockers like 'Spawn Again', and there is even a paean to disenfranchised youth in the crunchy 'Anthem for the Year 2000'. Yet, there is also a vulnerability and softness in the lyrics and musical arrangements of songs such as 'Miss You Love' and 'Ana's Song'. The latter chronicles Johns' contemporaneous battle with anorexia nervosa, which had become publicly evident in his skeletal physique. The Sydney Symphony Orchestra and acclaimed Australian pianist David Helfgott guest on the opening track, 'Emotion Sickness'.

Neon Ballroom didn't win everyone over. Neva Chonin (1999), writing in *Rolling Stone*, described the album as 'about what you'd expect from a young band going through its awkward stage' – a(nother) reference to both the band's youth and the record's assemblage of musical styles. I tend to agree that these styles do not gel as comfortably as they could have. Nonetheless, the record did otherwise receive hearty critical praise and signaled that the 'chair were not about to rest on their musical laurels.

The fourth album, *Diorama* (2002), opens with the lush 'Across the Night', which became the album's fifth single. This track sets the mood for much of what will come: hushed vocals, dreamy imagery, languid pace, orchestral arrangements. The group show a romantic side in 'Luv Your Life', the third single, and 'My Favourite Thing' that had largely been missing from previous albums. This whiff of romance might have an autobiographical component; Johns had been dating Australian singer-actress Natalie Imbruglia since 1999, and they would marry in 2003 (the marriage ended in 2008). And yes, there was an anthem in the form of the deliciously majestic The Greatest View from Here'.

Diorama has its pedestrian moments, and these come, interestingly enough, when the band attempt more straightforward, radio-friendly rock. 'The Lever' and 'One Way Mule' are two examples. Yet, the album overall was musically ambitious, and this ambition was rewarded by listeners. It entered the Australian music charts at the #1 position (ARIA 2021). There were positive reviews; for example, the *South Florida Sun-Sentinel* described the record as 'impervious to the rock staples of our contemporaries, a risky venture worth taking … marking the maturity of a prodigal band already wise beyond its years' (Calise 2003: 71). In 2007, the album was included in the SBS documentary series *Great Australian Albums*.

In other ways, *Diorama* is significant. It was during the period of this album's release that the band started capitalizing the 's' in 'Silverchair'. *Diorama* is the first of two albums from the band to be released in Australia by Eleven, John Watson's record label. The previous three albums had all been products of Murmur. The previous two albums had been produced by Nick Launay, whereas on *Diorama*, production duties were shared by Johns and Canadian producer John Bottrill. Johns told one interviewer:

> This was the first time I've ever done meetings with producers, because I knew that this was the kind of record that people were either going to be into or were really going to hate. . . . The majority of the people that I met prior to meeting David [Bottrill] either didn't understand it, or understood it and didn't like it and wanted to change it. They were all really supportive and nice, but I didn't feel like I was on the same page with anyone. (Cited in Farinella 2003)

Bottrill had an impeccable music pedigree, having worked with everyone from Toni Childs to Tool. Johns told one interviewer that 'as soon as I knew he was into [*Diorama*], I wanted him to do it because I knew that he makes things sound like gold' (cited in Farinella 2003).

Silverchair's final album to date, *Young Modern* (2007) was the second album to be released by Eleven. This record represents nothing so much as a marriage of power pop, glam rock and stadium anthems. There are touches of David Bowie on 'The Man Who Knew Too Much' and The Beatles on 'If You Keep Losing Sleep'. The first single, 'Straight Lines', is singalong material of the very best kind, with Johns sounding weary *and* upbeat.

Musically, the album represents a profound maturity on the band's behalf. Johns' vocals swoon delightfully through the ethereal 'Waiting All Day' and adopt Mick Jagger's sneering swagger in 'Mind Reader', the latter of which bears more than a slight resemblance to The Rolling Stones' 'Brown Sugar' (1971). There is top-notch playing from Gillies and Joannou and orchestral arrangements from Van Dyke Parks (who previously worked on *Diorama*). Judith Durham, lead singer of the beloved Australian folk group The Seekers, makes an appearance on 'English Garden', a charming slice of dream pop that was included on the iTunes release. Production duties are shared between Johns and Launay.

Reviews of *Young Modern* were largely positive, with critics praising its ambitiousness and the band's musical maturity (e.g. Zuel 2007). The album won six awards at the 2007 ARIAs: Best Group, Best Rock Album, Album of the Year, Single of the Year, Highest Selling Single and Best Video. The last three awards were for 'Straight Lines'. These wins brought the band's total number of ARIA Awards across their career to nineteen, which was the highest of any Australian act (Eastley and Turtle 2007).

Silverchair began work on their sixth album in 2009. Unfortunately, heavy drinking and tensions between band members stifled the assignment. This record remains unfinished.

No more tomorrows?

In July 2007, Silverchair performed 'Straight Lines' on *The Tonight Show with Jay Leno*. They'd been partying the previous evening and were worse for wear, a fact that could not be lost on the viewer. Johns' voice veers from raspy to non-existent; a doctor had warned him that performing that night might seriously damage his vocal cords, and it seems that this damage is happening in front of the television cameras (Gillies et al. 2023: 162). Yet, the boys keep on keeping on, pounding guitars and drums, howling throatily, until fade out.

I cite this anecdote because it nicely sums up Silverchair in their final decade: ploughing ahead through all manner of personal crises. There has been extensive media coverage of Johns' health problems, which also include a case of reactive arthritis that arose in the aftermath of recording *Diorama*. Johns would recall in 2022 that he endured 'bitterness and jealousy' in the band, with much of that jealousy coming from Gillies (cited in Cartwright 2022). In a 2023 podcast, Gillies opined that one reason for the tensions within the band was poor communication. He traced this poor communication to the stifling masculinity that pervaded their upbringing in Newcastle and that was discussed earlier in this book. In this time and place, boys were 'supposed to be as tough as nails and you don't talk about your feelings … there was a lot of stuff that went unsaid that should've been spoken about' (cited in Grynberg 2023). Gillies would himself battle with substance abuse and mental health challenges.

Eventually, in May 2011, Silverchair released a press statement announcing that they were taking an 'indefinite hibernation' (cited in Cartwright 2022). The 'brotherhood' that began in childhood would unravel in a very public fashion. There was a (since-healed) rift between Gillies and Joannou, although the major tension appears to have been between Gillies and Johns. Joannou recalls Johns saying: 'I'm sorry, man, but you're the kid stuck in the middle of a messy divorce' (cited in Gillies et al. 2023: 319).

In the ensuing years, Johns would remain in the spotlight with his two solo albums *Talk* (2015) and *FutureNever* (2022), both of which traversed rock, pop and R&B. He had already tested his music mettle outside Silverchair with his side project, The Dissociatives, a pop-oriented collaboration with Sydney DJ/producer Paul Mac that ran from approximately 2003 to 2005. In 2022, the singer told *Rolling Stone Australia/NZ* that he did not plan to undertake any more tours, explaining: 'The performance is fine; I'm totally cool to perform. It's the bit leading up to it. It drives me mental. It drives me crazy, I get so anxious' (cited in Lenke 2022).

In comparison, Joannou and Gillies have had much lower public profiles. Gillies continued with a number of music projects, including the solo EP *The Relative Relatives* in 2021.

Joannou largely departed the music industry, working for a time in hospitality, before moving into employment with the motorcycle business run by his wife's family. He has survived cancer and a heart attack. Joannou has written that for a long time, he 'felt like Silverchair wasn't my story to tell' (Gillies et al. 2023: 332). In 2023, Gillies and Joannou co-authored *Love and Pain: The Epic Times and Crooked Lines of Life Inside and Outside Silverchair* with Alley Pascoe. This book is the two men's attempt to tell their side of their band's story, from humble beginnings gigging around Newcastle to their unceremonious denouement. They would open up further in a two-part episode of ABC's current affairs program *Australian Story* that was screened in September 2023, coinciding with the book's publication (Cheshire 2023).[1]

As of July 2024, Joannou is based in Coffs Harbour, on New South Wales' north coast. Gillies and Johns both continue to reside in Newcastle, where the magic began all those years ago. The city has gentrified exponentially since the 1990s, and especially since 2008, when a social enterprise program called Renew Newcastle was launched. That program sought to 'revitalise the city centre through the letting of unused buildings, for peppercorn rents, as spaces for creatives to make and trade their wares' (Dickson 2022). Bars and eateries have sprung up around the city, while '[r]iverside wharves have been reborn as a lifestyle precinct' (Dickson 2022). The Cambridge Hotel, which we were introduced to in Chapter 1,

---

[1] Johns declined to be interviewed for this two-parter. Sony requested that the first part be removed from ABC iView (that station's streaming platform) because Johns had not consented to the use of silverchair's music (Israel 2023). The second part remains on iView as of 25 June 2024.

closed in 2023, but the city retains a vibrant live music scene (Wells 2024).

As for a Silverchair reunion – well, this seems unlikely, even considering the use of the non-conclusive word 'hiatus' in the 2011 statement. In 2021, Johns told the Australian current affairs program *The Project* that he would not reunite with his old band 'for a million dollars and with a gun to my head' (cited in Street 2021). This kind of statement sounds very final, though it's not guaranteed to provide anyone with closure. That is something that Gillies has expressed a desire for. He writes: 'We didn't get to do a farewell tour, or a greatest hits album, or a retrospective. We didn't get to say goodbye. It's like being frozen in suspended animation' (Gillies et al. 2023: 306).

Meanwhile, the band lives on in their influence on other bands and in memory. Let's have a look at some examples.

silverchair's influence

A great deal has been written in this book and elsewhere about *Frogstomp* borrowing from other acts, especially the Seattle grunge bands. In what follows, we'll survey three of the bands and artists that silverchair themselves influenced. This shows both the band's impact on Australian music and their ongoing legacy.

In the Introduction, I cited Ella Hooper's recollection of forming Killing Heidi with her brother Jesse. This is just one example of youngsters being inspired by Johns and co to start their own group. There are some interesting parallels between Heidi and silverchair. Both bands emerged in regional locations, with Heidi forming in Violet Town, situated in Victoria's northeast. Heidi hit it big in 1999 with their single 'Weir', which was released when Hooper was sixteen years old – around the same age as Johns, Gillies and Joannou when *Frogstomp* landed in record stores. Heidi merges rock and pop, much like silverchair, as well as folk music (Dwyer 2023). Hooper, like Johns, has achieved success within Australia as a solo artist.

Similar sentiments to Hooper's have been expressed by Kevin Parker of Perth psychedelic act Tame Impala. Parker remembers that he became a fan after discovering 1997's 'Freak':

> I saw the clip and they were quite young Australian dudes. 'It's not on the other side of the world, it's on the other side of the country, and they're only a little bit older than me – so if I work hard now, I can get where they are by the time I'm 15!' I was 11 or 12. (cited in Cooper 2015)

As it transpired, Parker was in his mid-twenties when Tame Impala released their first album, *Innerspeaker*, in 2010. Like silverchair, that act, of which Parker is the only regular member, went on to enjoy international success. Tame Impala has also earned the respect of none other than the 'chair's own frontman, who counts himself as a fan. In an episode of the *Who is Daniel Johns?* podcast, Johns recalls listening to 'Let It Happen' and thinking: 'Oh, shit, the game's changed . . . I thought that was such a bold artistic move' (2021: 'Daniel Talks to Kevin Parker'). 'Let It Happen' was the first single from Impala's *Currents* (2015) album and ran just shy of eight minutes, making it a lengthy track, indeed! Johns approvingly describes the choice of this track as lead single as being 'punk', which seems an apt choice of words when you consider how grunge music was an offshoot of punk music. In mentioning 'punk', Johns inadvertently hints at the genesis of the genre that his band's debut album has so commonly been associated with.

Finally, in 202', Australian surf rock band Hockey Dad expressed their admiration for silverchair in a contribution to *Rolling Stone Australia/NZ*'s '50 Greatest Australian Artists of All Time' series. The 'chair came eighth in this list. Hockey Dad's members, Billy Fleming and Zack Stephenson, recall how their families would remind them as teenagers that 'Silverchair hit the big time at your age, you know' (2021). Fleming and Stephenson recall: 'Being young scrappy kids growing up in a small rural town . . . it was insane to think that making records and touring the world could actually be possible for us' (2021).[2] Hockey Dad formed in Wollongong, which is located south of Sydney. I take the point being made, though I would point out that Wollongong, like Newcastle, is a city and not a town. Both locations would be difficult to truly classify as 'small'.[3]

---

[2] If this statement sounds familiar, that should be unsurprising; Ella Hooper has made a similar one, which I quoted in the Introduction.

[3] Wollongong 'covers a surface area of 572.2 kilometers squared' and has an estimated population of 315,379 ('Wollongong' 2024). Newcastle 'covers a total surface area of 261.8 kilometers squared' and has an estimated population of 465,145 ('Newcastle' 2024).

Remembering *Frogstomp*

So, let's circle back to *Frogstomp*. That album may not represent the entire sum of silverchair's career, but it sure was one helluva start. We'll revisit the debut record through the prism of memory.

The relationship between music and memory has been the subject of extensive scholarship and with good reason: it highlights one of the pivotal roles that music plays in constructing our sense of everyday life, of where we have been (physically, emotionally) and where we are now. Music researchers Andy Bennett and Ian Rogers write: 'Through their continuous pattern of encounter with mediations of the past – be these filmic, televisual, musical or "virtual" – individuals in contemporary society are perpetually in the process of remembering, and in the reflexive organization and articulation of their memories, in the present' (2016: 2). To illustrate, listening to *Frogstomp* again on Spotify after many years, I was transported back to my teenage bedroom, where that album played frequently on my boombox. I recalled the excitement of humming along to tracks and my parents smiling weakly at the aggressive lyrics.

As Catherine Strong points out in her book-length study of grunge music, 'memory is . . . highly subjective, and is constantly undergoing revision' (2011: 58). Memories can take on different emotional hues according to the distance from the remembered object, changes in personal taste and life circumstances. I recognize that my own *Frogstomp* memories are part of a 'romance with [my] own fantasy' of the past (Boym

2001: xiii). This fantasy neglects the more unglamorous aspects of my teenage life: my forced attempts at grunge fashion, the middling sound quality of that boombox, the skips on the cassette.

The mediatized remembering of silverchair has gained apace in recent years. This is doubtless due to a broader cultural nostalgia surrounding the 1990s and grunge music, as evidenced by a wave of media articles and public events such as 2017's 'Nostalgia is for losers', which was held in Seattle in December 2017 and which showcased grunge memorabilia (De May 2017), and by assorted social media accounts dedicated to the songs and sounds of that decade. There are several salient reasons behind 1990s nostalgia, which I'll divide into 'technological' and 'temporal', though there are overlaps between both.

Technological

The contemporary mediascape has provided fertile and expansive territory for the 1990s to be remembered, nostalgically and otherwise. This is a mediascape driven by and through what is sometimes called 'Web 2.0'. Web 2.0 emerged around the mid-2000s and spans

> all connected devices; Web 2.0 applications are those that make the most of the intrinsic advantages of that platform: delivering software as a continually-updated service that gets better the more people use it, consuming and remixing data from multiple sources, including individual users, while providing their own data and services in a form that allows remixing by others, creating network effects through an

'architecture of participation', and going beyond the page metaphor of Web 1.0 to deliver rich user experiences. (Cited in Fuchs 2011: 288)

As this quote suggests, Web 2.0 enables the kind of user participation that was impossible during the era of Web 1.0, which entailed 'a network of pages tied together by hyperlinks interconnected in a self-referencing mesh' (cited in Thompson and Weldon 2022: ix). Social networking sites (SNS) allow users from across the world to connect and celebrate shared interests – in other words, establish 'imagined communities'. SNS and other online platforms provide the tools and software to upload content (videos, interviews) that might otherwise have been consigned to history.

Put simply, then, Web 2.0 is a space where the boundaries between producer and consumer are blurring into an entity commonly known as the 'prosumer'; anyone with internet access can produce their own pop culture tributes, be it in the form of videos, podcasts or long-form essays published on blogs. Web 2.0 is also a space which, due to its boundless scope, can host and store more content than any piece of 'heritage' media (e.g. hard copy magazines and newspapers, CDs, cassette tapes) ever could.

When you log onto the net, you'll find silverchair tributes that range from the earnest to the hilarious. A personal favourite has been the @1994DanielJohns account on X (formerly Twitter). This account was established in June 2022 and features comical posts authored from the perspective of a pseudo-fifteen-year-old Daniel Johns. I write 'pseudo' because this is not the work of Johns himself; the author (who remains anonymous) acknowledges in a 22 August 2023 tweet that the tweets are parodic. The tweets reference actual people and events, for example: 'Do you guys reckon Frogstomp is a good name for an album? Label thinks it sucks, we think it's cool?' (17 July 2022); 'Today we start recording the album with Caveman. Heaps excited!' (23 December 2023).

The account also posts everyday observations that a 1990s Daniel Johns might well have been making had X been available back then, for example, 'Band practice gonna be awkward as fuck today' (5 July 2022); 'Mad magazine is hell funny' (10 July 2022). Such posts provide opportunities for silverchair fans old and new to laugh along with familiar anecdotes, written in a facsimile of Johns' laconic 1990s vocal style, and to remember the first year of that band's success. This is a very in-group humour. Non-fans, and those unfamiliar with the finer details of the band's early years, may find the references opaque.

I also want to give a shout-out to the Web 2.0 affordances that have enabled the writing of this book. For example, the streaming platform YouTube hosts recordings of silverchair performances throughout their career. I could revisit the music videos and the ARIA (non-)appearances many years after watching them on TV. Podcasts such as *Who is Daniel Johns?* (2021) and *Too Much of Not Enough* (2020–21) have provided comprehensive insights into the band's early years. These insights have frequently been delivered by way of interviews with key folk: the band members, John Watson and fans such as Kevin Parker.

Temporal

I'm not a betting man, but nevertheless, I would wager that 1990s nostalgia is especially acute for GenXers. These GenXers are now in their forties and fifties; they will have jobs, mortgages or rent, perhaps even children of their own to worry about. What could be more irresistible than reflecting on a worry-free youth? However, 1990s nostalgia is also appealing to young people who did not live through that decade. Through Spotify and social media, these youngsters can enjoy pop culture highlights of a time they would have only heard about (Hogarty 2016: 42). This kind of enjoyment is not, of course, new; think about the young Ben Gillies rocking out to his video copy of a 1971 Led Zeppelin concert.

Further, for all their darker moments, the 1990s at least seems like a less complex time than the present. Neil Ewen argues that 'an imaginative return to [that decade] is attractive and affectively powerful amid rising inequality and the rampant disorientation of the present', not to mention the contemporary pressure to be always connected via social media (2020: 577). The 1990s was definitely a simpler era in terms of music distribution and consumption, as John Watson suggests in a 2019 interview:

> You've still got all the old [media outlets], you've still got the Rolling Stone, you've still got The Courier Mail, you've still got 4MMM, but now you've also got Vodafone and you've got Channel V and you've got Facebook and Twitter and Faster Louder and Mess and Noise and an endless proliferation of channels. (cited in Graham 2019: 69)

In this panoply of media outlets and platforms, 'you've got three times as many boxes to tick to reach the same number of people' as in the days that silverchair hit it big (cited in Graham 2019: 69). True, today's up-and-coming bands can attract a following using Instagram and YouTube, but they're also battling for attention with a plethora of other bands promoting themselves on heritage and social media.

Finally, *Frogstomp*, the album, turned twenty in 2015. This birthday was celebrated by the release of a remastered version of the album. A number of review articles were published, discussing *Frogstomp* and (re)evaluating the content. Other writers joined in the recollections in the years that followed, as did the band members themselves.

Let's dive in and hear what these folks have to say.

Critics remember Frogstomp

Alex Sievers (2015) wrote that the remastered record 'really amplifies the band's growing potential (and the level of Johns' guitars)' as they were back in 1995. Sievers stated that songs such as 'Tomorrow' and 'Israel's Son' 'really are the testament of this band, their skill and potential at such a young age' (2015). Colm Browne (2015) echoes this sentiment about the band's talent, which belied their youth, writing that the album may seem 'a little raw and basic', but that it 'paved the way for a wonderful career'. Pearl HQ (2015) similarly opines that *Frogstomp* 'remains an early indication of the even greater success yet to come'.

Some critics noted the distinctly 1990s nature of the album. This was expressed in mostly favourable terms. Caz

Tran and Sam Wicks wrote in 2021 that 'you couldn't get a purer generational timestamp than *Frogstomp*'. A year earlier, Matthew Wand (2020) wrote that the record 'still passes the test of time. Like many albums released in the early to mid 90's they sound as fresh and relevant as they did back then'.

Yes, *Frogstomp* has some cringeworthy lines. In saying that, one reviewer did praise the album's 'lyrical maturity', while more recent writers have expressed similar sentiments. James Rose (2015) acknowledges the 'lyrical intensity' of songs like 'Israel's Son', which made the band sound much older than they actually were. Rose (2015) especially praised 'Tomorrow', acknowledging that while some passages were 'clunky', it provided a fierce 'rant at inequality, political ineptitude, injustice and pending revolution'. Rose echoes Browne (2015), who wrote: 'The writing shows a want to question the world, express feelings, get rid of negatives and be positive.' This shift from negative to positive, darkness to light, has been an under-remarked but remarkable aspect of the record, as we saw in Chapter 2.

Some recent critics acknowledged that *Frogstomp* played a pivotal role in their musical awakening. For them, the album has become an object of gratitude as well as nostalgia. Browne (2015) writes:

Released way back when I was 13 years old, it was one of the very first albums that brought out my love for rock music. Being a little too young to have appreciated Nirvana and the other late 80's and early 90's Seattle bands myself, this was my avenue into the world of grunge and teenage angst.

Glen Bushell (2015) recalls purchasing the album around a year after its initial release and wrote that a 'warm sense of nostalgia' made reviewing the twentieth anniversary reissue 'a thoroughly enjoyable excursion'. Bushell also writes that *Frogstomp* is 'a great document that shows how this little rock band from New South Wales cut their teeth to become one of Australia's biggest exports' (2015).

silverchair remember Frogstomp

This section asks: How do those band members remember their debut album? Not fondly, or at least this is what I had initially suspected Prior to writing this book, I knew that on tours after 1999, the band largely avoided songs from their first EP (Hedger 2021). And, of course, I had read all about their acrimonious split.

A closer look reveals a more complex picture.

Let's start with Daniel Johns. In a 2015 interview to commemorate *Frogstomp*'s twentieth anniversary, Johns said:

> My biggest obstacle [as an artist] was being pigeonholed, especially in America, as the guy from Silverchair that wrote *Frogstomp* when he was 14 years old. I feel like I worked really f---ing hard to get away from that. I'm proud of the fact that I never really exploited that part of myself and I always pushed myself to be a better writer. (cited in Armstrong 2015)

This is a perfectly reasonable statement. silverchair were still in their teens when they released their first record; they had yet to experiment with and diversify their sound in the ways they did with their subsequent albums. And hell, who wants their lives to be defined by the antics of their teenage self?

In that same interview, though, Johns does say: 'The songwriting might not be genius, but I think sonically, the performances [on *Frogstomp*] are really good. It's really honest; it's just three Australian kids thrashing it out in the studio and that's exactly how it sounds' (cited in Armstrong 2015). This implies that the singer does have affection for the record. He certainly, and understandably, seems to feel a sense of ownership towards it. In 2021, Kevin Shirley told *Who is Daniel Johns?* that he 'made' *Frogstomp*. Johns responded by acknowledging the producer's important work but emphasizing that the record was very much his band's creation (Hyland 2021).

Like Johns, Gillies and Joannou appear to have largely warm memories of the LP, with Gillies telling an interviewer in 2020:

> It was a really exciting time when *Frogstomp* came out and everything just went berserk. We went and did some shows and people were going bananas. . . . We were just three dudes from New Castle [sic] playing music and having a great time. Years later, like now, you kind of realize what kind of effect you had on people's lives. That's pretty awesome, to be just a pivotal point in people's lives and be that musical reference point for people to look back on. (cited in Gorra 2020).

Gillies here acknowledges that *Frogstomp* did not just entertain 1990s audiences; it has become indelibly associated in the public memory with that point in time. He's absolutely correct. When I recall that decade, it's the music, including silverchair's debut album, that springs immediately to mind.

Speaking for myself

My reverence for *Frogstomp* is intertwined with my unceasing fondness for the year in which it was released. In 1995, I was a teenager living a comfortable middle-class suburban life with unlimited free time and no commitments save for high school. University, bills and paid employment were still a few years off. silverchair's first album was the soundtrack to that year, and, of course, I wished those twelve months would last forever.

Unfortunately, wishes don't always come true.

I recall being underwhelmed by *Freak Show* upon its release, finding tracks such as 'Freak' and 'Abuse Me' almost unbearably corny. Somehow, I overlooked the naffness of certain *Frogstomp* lyrics. I recall finding *Neon Ballroom* too sombre, although of course the 1995 record was hardly a celebration of lightness and joy. I didn't mind *Diorama* and *Young Modern* when both were released, but by that stage, I'd accepted that the silverchair I enjoyed as a high schooler was no more.

In hindsight, my lukewarm reactions to the subsequent albums might have reflected my unease that silverchair were moving away from their initial 'grunge' sound and, y'know, evolving as a band. Maybe I was also reacting to the passing of the 'grunge moment' and the carefree time in my life that this moment coincided with. Maybe I just wanted to be stuck in 1994–5 forever, with the equally raw and guileless sounds of *Frogstomp* as my forever soundtrack.

I was certainly pigeonholing silverchair as grungers, and this was the very thing that Daniel Johns did not want to happen.

Writing this book has enriched my appreciation of silverchair's musical journey and talent. *Frogstomp* marks a dynamic beginning to that journey, the kind that most garage musos can only dream of, and the band would continue to evolve in the sixteen years that followed. Yes, the record has moments of cringe, but how many fifteen-year-olds sound as ferocious as the 'chair did?

This book will hopefully also contribute to public understanding of the significant role that *Frogstomp* plays in the history of Australian music. The silverchair of 1995 sounded a lot like Pearl Jam, but their music contained Australian and international influences that went over my teenage head – and evidently the heads of a few reviewers, too! The band's global success is especially impressive when you consider that they were based outside urban Australia, the latter being the site of many music tours and of the music companies that fashion Australian listening tastes. silverchair attracted big names in the Australian music industry to work with them – the two Johns, Kevin Shirley – while their star was only beginning to rise. silverchair would themselves influence later bands, just as they'd been influenced by grunge gurus, Black Sabbath and Led Zeppelin.

Frogstomp may indeed be a product of its era, but it's also an album that continues to be remembered and enjoyed today and will doubtless be enjoyed tomorrow.

References

Albury, K. (1999), 'Spaceship Triple J: Making the National Youth Network'. *Media International Australia*, 91(1): 55–66.

Ali, L. (1995), 'Silverchair: The Kids Are Alright; Pop Music Review: Teen Band, Known for its Cuteness as Well as its Music, is Surprisingly Dynamic in Person'. *Los Angeles Times*, 14 September: 1.

Anderson, B. (1983), *Imagined Communities: Reflections on the Origins and Spread of Nationalism*. Revised Edition. London and New York: Verso.

Appadurai, A. (1996), *Modernity at Large: Cultural Dimensions of Globalization*. Minnesota: University of Minnesota Press.

Apter, J. (2013), *Up from Down Under: How Australian Music Changed the World*. Victoria: The Five Mile Press.

Apter, J. (2018), *The Book of Daniel: From Silverchair to Dreams*. New South Wales: Allen & Unwin.

Apter, J. (2020), 'How "Easyfever" Affected George Young & The Easybeats Revealed In New Biography'. *The Music*, 4 August. https://themusic.com.au/news/george-young-easybeats -friday-my-mind-biography-jeff-apter/tlWspqmoq6o/04-08 -20 (accessed 20 July 2024).

ARIA. (2021), 'All The ARIA Albums Chart #1s'. *ARIA*, 23 February. https://www.aria.com.au/charts/news/all-the-aria-albums -chart-1s (accessed 7 June 2024).

Armstrong, C. (2015), 'Daniel Johns Reflects on "Frogstomp" + Shares His Thoughts on a Silverchair Reunion'. *Diffuser*, 28 May.

Available online: https://diffuser.fm/silverchair-daniel-johns
-frogstomp-interview-2015/ (accessed 5 February 2024).

Arrow, M. (2009), *Friday on our Minds: Popular Culture in Australia
since 1945*. New South Wales: University of New South Wales
Press.

Attfield, N. (2023), *Lamestains: Grunge, Sub Pop and the Music of
the Loser*. London: Reaktion Books.

Auslander, P. (2023), *Liveness: Performance in a Mediatized Culture*.
Third Edition. London and New York: Routledge.

Azerrad, M. (1992), 'Nirvana: Inside the Heart and Mind of Kurt
Cobain'. *Rolling Stone*, 16 April. Available online: https://www
.rollingstone.com/music/music-news/nirvana-inside-the-heart
-and-mind-of-kurt-cobain-2-235093/ (accessed 4 April 2024).

Baroni, N. (2014), 'Watch Guns N Roses' Tribute To Doc Neeson'.
Music Feeds, 6 June. https://musicfeeds.com.au/news/watch
-guns-n-roses-tribute-to-doc-neeson/ (accessed 13 July
2024).

Bennett, A., and Rogers, I. (2016), *Popular Music Scenes and
Cultural Memory*. London: Springer Nature.

Bennett, R. (2015), 'Live Concerts and Fan Identity in the Age of
the Internet'. In A. Jones, J. Bennett, and R. J. Bennett (Eds), *The
Digital Evolution of Life Music*, 3–15. Surrey, England: Ashgate.

Bester, C. (1995), 'Debut Success: Review of *Frogstomp*'. *Port
Lincoln Times*, 22 June: 35.

Billboard 200. (undated), 'Silverchair', Date of Posting Unknown.
https://www.billboard.com/artist/silverchair/ (accessed 28
July 2024).

Boym, S. (2001), *The Future of Nostalgia*. New York: Basic Books.

Bracknell, C., and Barwick, L. (2020), 'The Fringe or the Heart
of Things? Aboriginal and Torres Strait Islander Musics in
Australian Music Institutions'. *Musicology Australia*, 42(2):
70–84.

Bristow, J (2015), *Baby Boomers and Generational Conflict.* Hampshire and New York: Palgrave Macmillan.

Brown, S. C., and Knox, D. (2017), 'Why Go to Pop Concerts? The Motivations Behind Live Music Attendance'. *Musicae Scientiae*, 21(3): 233–249.

Browne, C. (2015), 'Silverchair – 20th Anniversary of Frogstomp Review'. *Soundscape*, 22 June. Available online: https://www .soundscapemagazine.com/silverchairfrogstomp/ (accessed 4 February 2024).

Burke, G., and Egar, R. (2020), 'Ross Knight, an Aussie Veteran of the Grunge Era, Saw Pearl Jam's Rise Up Close'. *Double J*, 10 September. Available online: https://www.abc.net.au/listen /doublej/music-reads/features/cosmic-psychos-ross-knight -saw-pearl-jams-rise-up-close/12648448 (accessed 4 April 2024).

Bushell, G. (2015), 'Silverchair – 'Frogstomp: 20th Anniversary'. *Punktastic*, 8 July. Available online: http://www.punktastic .com/album-reviews/silverchair-frogstomp-20th-anniversary/ (accessed 3 February 2024).

Calise, A. (2003), 'Silverchair Grows Up'. *South Florida Sun-Sentinel*, 3 January: 71.

Cartwright, L. (2022), 'Why Daniel Johns' Decision to Quit Silverchair Broke Years-long Friendship'. *News.com.au*, 2 September. Available online: https://www.news.com.au/ entertainment/music/why-daniel-johns-decision-to-quit -silverchair-broke-yearslong-friendship/news-story/8bf9bd3 c53160202add67b8ec7dc0758 (accessed 4 February 2024).

Chalmers, S. (2020), 'History Suggests Youth Unemployment Will Surge, Pain Will Last a Decade after Coronavirus Crisis'. *ABC News*, 16 April. https://www.abc.net.au/news/2020 -04-16/history-suggests-youth-unemployment-will-surge -coronavirus/12151668 (accessed 17 May 2024).

Chonin, N. (1999), 'Review of *Neon Ballroom*'. *Rolling Stone*, 18 March. https://www.rollingstone.com/music/music-album-reviews/neon-ballroom-250324/ (accessed 6 June 2024).

Christgau, R. (1995), 'Consumer Guide'. *Village Voice*, 28 November: 52.

Connell, R. W. (2005), *Masculinities*. Second Edition. California: University of California Press.

Cooper, L. (2015), 'Tame Impala's Kevin Parker On The Soundtrack Of His Life'. *NME*, 13 August. https://www.nme.com/blogs/nme-blogs/tame-impalas-kevin-parker-on-the-soundtrack-of-his-life-15968?utm_source=twitter&utm_medium=social (accessed 1 June 2024).

Davies, N. (2014), 'RIP Bernard "Doc" Neeson: We're Never Gonna See that Face Again'. *The Advertiser*, 4 June. Available online: https://www.adelaidenow.com.au/news/south-australia/rip-bernard-doc-neeson-were-never-gonna-see-that-face-again/news-story/00538a6f29d2fd7f61b4fafbde0d7f75 (accessed 4 March 2024).

Davis, M. (1997), *Gangland: Cultural Elites and the New Generationalism*. New South Wales: Allen and Unwin.

De May, D. (2017), 'Nostalgia is for Losers' Shows Off Relics of '90s Grunge Era'. *Seattle PI*, 11 December. Available online: https://www.seattlepi.com/seattlenews/article/Grunge-exhibit-Seattle-Nirvana-Soundgarden-12422309.php (accessed 25 February 2024).

Deniztek. (undated), 'Radio Birdman, New Race (1977)'. *Deniztek*, date of posting unknown. https://www.deniztek.com/rb-new-race-7 (accessed 27 July 2024).

Dickson, M. (2022), 'A Love Letter to Newcastle: New Century, New Vision'. *The Guardian Australia*, 6 February. https://www.theguardian.com/australia-news/2022/feb/06/a-love-letter-to-newcastle-new-century-new-vision (accessed 19 August 2024).

Dwyer, M. (2023), '"I Wanted Out": Ella Hooper on Fame, Loss,
     and Killing Off Heidi'. *The Sydney Morning Herald*, 12 January.
     https://www.smh.com.au/culture/music/i-wanted-out-ella
     -hooper-on-fame-loss-and-killing-off-heidi-20230105-p5caky
     .html (accessed 1 June 2024).
Eliezer, C. (1995), 'The New Guard Rises from Down Under'.
     Billboard, 30 September: 65–66.
Eltham, B. (2009), 'The Curious Significance of Triple j'. *Meanjin*,
     68(3). https://meanjin.com.au/essays/the-curious-significance
     -of-triple-j/ (accessed 27 August 2024).
English, H. J., Monk, S., and Davidson, J. W. (2018), 'Music and
     World-building in Newcastle, New South Wales, Australia'.
     International Journal of Community Music, 11(3): 245–264.
Evans, M. (1998), '"Quality" Criticism: Music Reviewing in
     Australian Rock Magazines'. *Perfect Beat*, 3(4): 38–50.
Ewen, N. (2020), '"Talk to Each Other Like It's 1995": Mapping
     Nostalgia for the 1990s in Contemporary Media Culture'.
     Television & New Media, 21(6): 574–580.
Farinella, D. J. (2003), 'Silverchair'. *Mix*, 1 January. https://web
     .archive.org/web/20120217010922/http://mixonline.com/
     recording/interviews/audio_silverchair/ (accessed 23 June
     2024).
Fleming, B., and Stephenson, Z. (2021), '50 Greatest Australian
     Artists of All Time – #8: Silverchair'. *Rolling Stone Australia/NZ*,
     19 February. https://au.rollingstone.com/music/music
     -features/50-greatest-australian-artists-of-all-time-silverchair
     -22949/ (accessed 1 June 2024).
Fox, J., and Doyle, E. (2018), 'Public Flashing, Topless Performances
     and Even Thanking Drug Dealers: A Look Back at the ARIAs
     Most Outrageous Moments ahead of the Australian Music
     Industry's Night of Nights'. *Daily Mail Australia*, 28 November.
     https://www.dailymail.co.uk/tvshowbiz/article-6436125/

The-ARIA-Awards-outrageous-jaw-dropping-moments.html
(accessed 13 June 2024).

Fricke, D. (1996), 'Silverchair: Boy's Life'. *Rolling Stone*, 22 February.
https://www.rollingstone.com/music/music-news/silverchair
-boys-life-48313/4/ (accessed 17 February 2024).

Fricke, D. (1998), 'Frogstomp'. *Rolling Stone*, 2 February. Available
online: https://www.rollingstone.com/music/music-album
-reviews/frogstomp-250249/ (accessed 7 November 2023).

Frith, S. (2007), 'Live Music Matters'. *Scottish Music Review*, 1(1): 1–17.

Fuchs, C. (2011), 'Web 2.0, Prosumption, and Surveillance'.
Surveillance & Society, 8(3): 288–309.

Galuszka, P., and Wyrzykowska, K. M. (2019), 'Rethinking
Independence: What Does "Independent Record Label"
Mean Today?' In L. Gillon, E. Mazierska, and T. Rigg (Eds),
*Popular Music in the Post-Digital Age: Politics, Economy, Culture
and Technology*, 33–49. New York and London: Bloomsbury
Academic.

Giles, D. (2023), 'Defining Parasocial Relationship Experiences'.
In R. T. Forster (Ed.), *The Oxford Handbook of Parasocial
Experiences*, 33–50. New York: Oxford University Press.

Gillies, B., Joannou, C., and Pascoe, A. (2023), *Love & Pain: The Epic
Times and Crooked Lines of Life Inside and Outside Silverchair*.
New South Wales: Hatchette Australia.

Givens, R. (1996), 'Review of Frogstomp'. *Stereo Review*, 16(2): 142.

Goodwin, M. (2018), 'Screen Circuits: Fear and Paranoia in the
Sprawl (circa 1995)'. *M/C Journal*, 21(5). https://journal.media
-culture.org.au/index.php/mcjournal/article/view/1488
(accessed 20 August 2024).

Gorra, J. (2020), 'Ben Gillies reflects upon Silverchair's Frogstomp
25 Years Later'. *Artist Waves*, 25 August. Available online:
https://artistwaves.com/ben-gillies-reflects-upon-silverchairs
-frogstomp-25-years-later-2/ (accessed 3 February 2024).

Graham, P. (2019), *Music, Management, Marketing and Law: Interviews Across the Music Business Value Chain*. Switzerland: Springer.

Groeneveld, J. (1998), *Growing the Hunter Contemporary/Popular Music Industry Feasibility Study*. Newcastle: HAC & DEWRSB.

Gross, E., and Musgrave, G. (2020), *Can Music Make You Sick? Measuring the Price of Musical Ambition*. London: University of Westminster Press.

Harvey, D. (2005), *A Brief History of Neoliberalism*. Oxford: Oxford University Press

Hawkins, R. (2014), '"Sheilas and Pooftas": Hyper-Heteromasculinity in 1970s Australian Popular Music Cultures'. *Limina*, 20(2): 85–98.

Hebdige, D. (1979), *Subculture: The Meaning of Style*. London: Methuen.

Hennessey, T. (2023), 'Where Were You? UK Chart Pop and the Commodification of the Teenage Libido 1952–1963'. *Let's Spend the Night Together: Sex, Pop music and British youth culture 1950s-80s*, 16–37. The Subcultures Network. Manchester: Manchester University Press.

Hill, R. L. (2014), 'Reconceptualizing Hard Rock and Metal Fans as a Group: Imaginary Community'. *International Journal of Community Music*, 7(2): 173–187.

Hogarty, J. (2016), *Popular Music and Retro Culture in the Digital Era*. New York and London: Routledge.

Holder, C. (2005), 'Cracking the USA'. *AudioTechnology*, 14 September. https://www.audiotechnology.com/features/cracking-the-usa (accessed 21 July 2024).

Holmes, P. (1995), 'Silence is Silver'. *The Sydney Morning Herald*, 8 October: 127.

Homan, S. (2003), *The Mayor's a Square: Live Music and Law and Order in Sydney*. New South Wales: Local Consumption Publications.

HQ, P. (2015), 'Silverchair - Frogstomp 20th Anniversary Edition'. *Pearl HQ*, 27 March. Available online: https://pearlhq.com.au /2015-03-silverchair-frogstomp-20th-anniversary-edition/ (accessed 3 February 2024).

Humphrys, E. (2018), *How Labour Built Neoliberalism : Australia's Accord, the Labour Movement and the Neoliberal Project*. Boston: Brill.

Hyland, J. (2021), 'Music Producer Claims He "Made" Silverchair's Debut Album Frogstomp because Daniel Johns and His Fellow Band Members Were Just 14 at the Time: "It Was My Baby, As Well as Theirs"'. *Daily Mail Australia*, 4 November. Available online: https://www.dailymail.co.uk/tvshowbiz /article-10163349/Silverchair-Daniel-Johns-denies-claim -producer-Frogstomp.html (accessed 4 February 2024).

Ihaza, J. (2017), 'Everyone is Stage Diving'. *The Outline*, 23 June. https://theoutline.com/post/1782/stage-diving-rappers-travis -scott-lil-uzi-vert (accessed 20 July 2024).

Israel, J. (2023), 'Daniel Johns Addresses Disagreement with Silverchair Bandmates after ABC Documentary Pulled from iView'. *The Guardian Australia*, 25 September. https://www .theguardian.com/music/2023/sep/25/daniel-johns-speaks -disagreement-silverchair-a-silver-lining-documentary -removed-abc-iview-why-instagram (accessed 25 June 2024).

Jenke, T. (2022), 'Daniel Johns: The Defiant One'. *Rolling Stone Australia/NZ*, 22 April. https://au.rollingstone.com/music/ music-features/daniel-johns-solo-album-interview-39052/ (accessed 1 June 2024).

Jolly, N. (2018), 'Australian Rock Star Daniel Johns' Darkest Days'. *News.com.au*, 2 December. https://www.news.com .au/entertainment/music/australian-rock-star-daniel-johns -darkest-days/news-story/0b6dee3b20613bfcea58242 cd2fd2c99 (accessed 11 March 2023).

Jones, A. (2015), 'What's My Scene: Festival Fandom and the Applification of the Big Day Out stage'. In A. Cresswell-Jones and R. J. Bennett (Eds), *The Digital Evolution of Live Music*, 29–40. Oxford: Chandos Publishing.

Kimbo (2015), 'Velvet Underground'. *History of Australian Music from 1960 until 2000*, 12 April. http://historyofaussiemusic.blogspot.com/2015/04/velvet-underground.html (accessed 18 April 2024).

Kot, G. (1995), 'Youthful Openers Silverchair Outbuzz Headliner Hum'. *Chicago Tribune*, 26 June: 12.

Lang, R. (1993), 'New Music Show on the Move'. *The Canberra Times*, 3 May: 38.

Mackay, H. (2024), 'Boomer and Bust'. *The Weekend Australian Magazine*, 11–12 May: 26–29.

Makkai, T., and McAllister, I. (1998), *Patterns of Drug Use in Australia, 1985–95*. Canberra: Commonwealth of Australia.

Mannheim, K. (2013), 'The Problem of Generations'. In P. Kecskemeti (Ed), *Essays on the Sociology of Knowledge*, 276–320. London: Routledge

Mathieson, C. (1999), 'The Kids in America'. *Juice: 1999 Yearbook*, 126–133.

McGuirk, P. M., and Rowe, D. (2001), "Defining Moments' and Refining Myths in the Making of Place Identity: The Newcastle Knights and the Australian Rugby League Grand Final'. *Australian Geographical Studies*, 39(1): 52–66.

McIntyre, P., and Sheather, G. (2013), 'The Newcastle Music Industry: An Ethnographic Study of a Regional Creative System in Action'. *International Journal of Music Business Research*, 2(2), 36–60.

McKenzie, S. (2010), 'Silverchair: No Complaints from the "Chair". In S. Sennett and S. Groth (Eds), *Off the Record: 25 Years of Music Street Press*, 223–225. Queensland: University of Queensland Press.

McNeice, A. (2010), 'Kevin Shirley: Distortion To Death Threats - Life In A Producer's Chair'. *Melodic Rock*, December. http://melodic-rock.com/interviews/kevinshirley-2010-Part1.html (accessed 29 March 2024).

Metcalfe, A. W. (1993), 'Mud and Steel, The Imagination of Newcastle'. *Labour History*, 64: 1–16.

Michelsen, M. (2015), 'Music Criticism and Taste Cultures'. In J. Shepherd and K. Devine (Eds), *The Routledge Reader on the Sociology of Music*, 211–219. New York: Routledge.

Moore, A. (2002), 'Authenticity as Authentication'. *Popular Music*, 21(2): 209–223.

Moore, R. (2005), 'Alternative to What? Subcultural Capital and the Commercialization of a Music Scene'. *Deviant Behavior*, 26(3): 229–252.

Morrow, G., and Beckett, J. (2022), 'The Changing Role and Function of Music Charts in the Contemporary Music Economy'. In G. Morrow, D. Nordgard, and K. Tschmuck (Eds), *Rethinking the Music Business: Music Contexts, Rights, Data, and COVID-19*, 239–260. Switzerland: Springer.

Mrad, M. (2022), 'Silverchair Frontman Daniel Johns Reveals he was Devastated When Two Teenagers Carried Out a Triple-murder after Being "Influenced By His Song"'. *Daily Mail Australia*, 30 August. https://www.dailymail.co.uk/tvshowbiz/article-11158339/Silverchair-Daniel-Johns-triple-murder-teens-influenced-songs.html (accessed 4 June 2024).

MTV News. (1995), 'Silverchair Singer's Black Day'. *MTV News*, 13 November. https://www.mtv.com/news/ftx5k7/silverchair-singers-black-day (accessed 24 May 2024).

'Newcastle'. *World Population Review*. https://worldpopulationreview.com/cities/australia/newcastle (accessed 26 August 2024).

Newstead, A. (2023), 'Remembering the Cambridge Hotel, Newcastle's Iconic Live Music Venue'. *Double J*, 20 June.

https://www.abc.net.au/listen/doublej/music-reads/features/
cambridge-hotel-farewell-iconic-newcastle-live-music-history
/102445646 (accessed 27 May 2024).

O'Donnell, J. (1991), 'All Their Desperate Harmony'. *Cold Chisel:
The 50th Anniversary Tour.* https://www.coldchisel.com/band
/history/all-their-desperate-harmony-by-john-odonnell/
(accessed 21 July 2024).

Oldham, P. (2013), "Suck More Piss": How the Confluence of Key
Melbourne-based Audiences, Musicians, and Iconic Scene
Spaces Informed the Oz Rock Identity'. *Perfect Beat*, 14(2):
120–139.

Oldham, P. (forthcoming), '"There's Gonna be a Showdown":
Australian Pub Rock in the 1980s to Early 90s'. In Bennett, A.
and Stratton, J. (Eds), *Pub Rock in the UK* and Australia. London
and New York: Routledge.

Petridis, A. (2010), 'Peter Christopherson Obituary'. *The Guardian*,
29 November. Available online: https://www.theguardian
.com/music/2010/nov/28/peter-christopherson-obituary
(accessed 13 October 2024).

Polcz, S. (2023), 'Loyalties v. Royalties'. *Hastings LJ*, 74(3): 765–822.

Queenan, J. (2007), 'Was Smells Like Teen Spirit Really Named
after a Deodorant?' *The Guardian*, 19 July. https://www
.theguardian.com/music/2007/jul/19/popandrock.nirvana
(accessed 17 August 2024).

Quinn, K. (2024), 'Splendour's Cancellation Will Send Shockwaves
through Australia's Music Industry'. *The Age*, 28 March.
Available online: https://www.theage.com.au/culture/music
/splendour-s-cancellation-will-send-shockwaves-through
-australia-s-music-industry-20240327-p5ffqr.html (accessed
29 March 2024).

Ragusa, P. (2021), 'Moshing: The Art and Consequences of One of
the Most Celebrated Concert Dance Forms'. *Consequence*, 19

August. Available online: https://consequence.net/2021/08/ moshing-history-essay/ (accessed 20 July 2024).

Rhodes, C., and Pullen, A. (2012), 'Commercial Gender: Fracturing Masculinity in the Case of OzRock'. *Culture and Organization*, 18(1): 33–49.

Rodriguez, D. (2014), 'The N of Terror. Nasenbluten and the Cult of Bloody Fist Records'. *Vice*, 17 October. https://www.vice .com/en/article/the-n-of-terror-nasenbluten-and-the-cult-of -bloody-fist-records/ (accessed 14 October 2024).

Rogers, I., and Whiting, S. (2020), '"If There Isn't Skyscrapers, Don't Play There!" Rock Music Scenes, Regional Touring, and Music Policy in Australia'. *Popular Music and Society*, 43(4): 450–460.

Rose, J. (2015), '20 Years Since: Silverchair's Frogstomp'. *Daily Review*, 30 October. Available online: https://dailyreview .com.au/20-years-since-silverchairs-frogstomp/ (accessed 3 February 2024).

Saunders, D. (1995), 'Never Too Young to Rock With the Best'. *The Age*, 20 April: 18.

Savage, J. (2007), *Teenage: The Creation of Youth Culture*. New York: Viking.

Scribner, S. (1997), 'Review of Silverchair, "Freak Show"'. *Los Angeles Times*, 2 February. Accessed via ProQuest (4 June 2024).

Scully, A. (1999), 'Silverchair Fan Wins Web Award'. *Llama Appreciation Society Website*, 11 August. Available online: https://15min.org/articles/1999/august/11/ootm_3.html (accessed 25 July 2024).

Scully, A., and Millington, B. (2019), 'Lost Tapes from Newcastle's Star Hotel Riot Resurface in New Documentary Series'. *ABC News*, 20 September. https://www.abc.net.au/news/2019-09 -20/new-documentary-series-launched-with-lost-vision-from -newcastle/11529034 (accessed 29 July 2024).

Shoebridge, N. (1995), 'SBS Moves to Bring the Bacon Back Home, Too'. *Australian Financial Review*, 13 March. https://www.afr .com/companies/sbs-moves-to-bring-the-bacon-back-home -too-19950313-kawqi (accessed 4 June 2024).

Shoebridge, N. (1996), 'Strategies Put Silverchair Into the Box Seat'. *Australian Financial Review*, 8 April. https://www.afr .com/companies/strategies-put-silverchair-into-the-box-seat -19960408-kayi7 (accessed 21 June 2024).

Silverchair Concert History. https://www.concertarchives.org/ bands/silverchair?page=23#concert-table (accessed 5 April 2024).

Silverpram. (1994), 'Tomorrow'. Available online: https://www .youtube.com/watch?v=cJRw6Rzun8w (accessed 1 April 2024).

Sievers, A. (2015), 'Album Review: Silverchair - 'Frogstomp (20th Anniversary Deluxe Edition)'. *The Music*, 21 April. Available online: https://themusic.com.au/reviews/silverchair -frogstomp-20th-anniversary-deluxe-edition/nl-6sLOytbQ/21 -04-15 (accessed 4 February 2024).

Soulsby, D. (2015), 'Corporate Rock Still Sucks: The Wild Sounds of SST in 10 Records'. *Vinyl Factory*, 1 September. Available online: https://thevinylfactory.com/features/corporate-rock -still-sucks-the-wild-sounds-of-sst-in-10-records/ (accessed 13 October 2024).

Stafford, A. (2018), 'The Grunge Effect: Music, Fashion, and the Media During the Rise of Grunge Culture In the Early 1990s'. *M/C Journal*, 21(5). https://journal.media-culture.org.au/index .php/mcjourna /article/view/1471 (accessed 13 July 2024).

Stafford, A. (2024), Radio Birdman on Their Last Shows – and Their Legacy: 'It's a Bit of a Wank to Acknowledge All That". *The Guardian*, 29 January. https://www.theguardian.com/music

/2024/jan/29/radio-birdman-australian-band-final-live-tour (accessed 17 August 2024).

Stapleton, D. (2014), 'Silverchair – Tomorrow: The Song that Blew Open Australian Rock'. *The Guardian,* 8 July. Available online: https://www.theguardian.com/music/australia-culture-blog /2014/jul/08/silverchair-tomorrow-the-song-that-blew-open -australian-rock (accessed 30 March 2024).

Starke, P., Kaasch, A., and van Hooren, F. (2013), *The Welfare State as Crisis Manager: Explaining the Diversity of Policy Responses to Economic Crisis.* Hampshire and New York: Palgrave Macmillan.

Stratton, J. (2007a), *Australian Rock: Essays on Popular Music.* Perth: Network Books.

Stratton, J. (2007b), 'Constructing an Avant-garde: Australian Popular Music and the Experience of Pleasure'. *Popular Music History*, 2(1): 49–75

Street, A. P. (2021), 'Who is Daniel Johns? The Hit Podcast Untangling Silverchair's Enigmatic Frontman'. *The Guardian*, 5 November. Available online: https://www.theguardian.com /music/2021/nov/05/who-is-daniel-johns-the-hit-podcast -untangling-silverchairs-enigmatic-frontman (accessed 3 February 2024).

Street, J. (2014), 'Awards, Prizes and Popular Taste: Organising the Judgement of Music'. In L. Marshall and D. Laing (Eds), *Popular Music Matters: Essays in Honour of Simon Frith*, 181–194. Surrey and Burlington, VT: Ashgate.

Strong, C. (2011), *Grunge: Music and Memory*. London and New York: Routledge.

Strong, C. (2013), 'The Contradictions of the Mainstream: Australian Views of Grunge and Commercial Success'. In S. Baker, A. Bennett, and J. Taylor (Eds), *Redefining Mainstream Popular Music*, 75–85. New York: Routledge.

Strong, C., and Rogers, I. (2016), 'She-riffs: Gender and the Australian Experience of Alternative Rock and Riot grrrl in the 1990s'. *Journal of World Popular Music*, 3(1): 38–53.

Sydney Morning Herald (SMH). (2002), 'I Woke Up and Couldn't Walk: Silvercha r Star'. *The Sydney Morning Herald*, 1 April. https://www.smh.com.au/entertainment/music/i-woke-up-and-couldnt-walk-silverchair-star-20020401-gdf5tc.html (accessed 26 July 2024).

Talbot, D. (1996), 'Rock Band Denies Role in US Murder'. *The Age*, 20 January: 3.

Taysom, J. (2020), 'This is Why Neil Young is Called the "Godfather of Grunge"'. *Far Out Magazine*, 18 August. https://faroutmagazine.co.uk/neil-young-godfather-grunge-kurt-cobain-eddie-vedder/ (accessed 17 May 2024).

Te Koha, N. (1995a), 'Silverchair Sits Out Awards'. *Herald Sun*, 3 October: 11.

Te Koha, N. (1995b), 'Get Out of Your Chair'. *Herald Sun*, 4 October: 13.

Testa, J. (1995), 'Review of Frogstomp'. *Chairpage*, October. Available online: http://www.chairpage.com/_news/archive/1995/oct07.htm (accessed 25 March 2024).

Thompson, J. D., and Weldon, J. (2022), *Content Production for Digital Media: An Introduction*. Singapore: Springer.

Thornton, S. (1995), *Club Cultures: Music, Media and Subcultural Capital*. Cambr dge: Polity.

Tran, C., and Wicks, S. (2021), 'Silverchair Delivered a Thrilling Synthesis of Rage, Confusion and Pain on Their Debut'. *Double J*, 20 September. Available online: https://www.abc.net.au/listen/doublej/music-reads/features/silverchair-frogstomp/13549562?fbclid=IwAR0Q_95gyF4xZuMYrtpO_a2NvHJK9WAMZCPFZ5uPnP-r9gNxEAKqqSmCzlY (accessed 4 February 2024).

Tsitsos, W. (1999), 'Rules of Rebellion: Slamdancing, Moshing, and the American Alternative Scene'. *Popular Music*, 18(3): 397–414.

Tsioulakis, I., and Hyton-Ng, E. (2016), *Musicians and Their Audiences : Performance, Speech and Mediation*. London and New York: Routledge.

Turnman, J. (1995), 'Silverchair – Teens Love the Viper … and We Don't Mean the Viper Room!' *BAM Magazine*, 20 October. Available online: https://www.chairpage.com/press_releases/item/15/ (accessed 29 December 2023).

Tzioumakis, Y., and Lincoln, S. (2019), *Rock Around the Clock: Exploitation, Rock'n'roll and the Origins of Youth Culture*. New York: Routledge.

Wand, M. (2020), 'Silverchair: The Story of Their Rise to Fame and Debut Album 'Frogstomp''. *Vinyl Chapters*, 25 February. Available online: https://www.vinylchapters.com/silverchair -the-story-of-their-rise-to-fame/ (accessed 4 February 2024).

Wells, S. (2024), 'The Ultimate Newcastle Gig Guide'. *Newcastle Weekly*, 21 June. https://newcastleweekly.com.au/the -ultimate-newcastle-gig-guide/ (accessed 25 June 2024).

Winchester, H. P. (1999), 'Lone Fathers and the Scales of Justice: Renegotiating Masculinity After Divorce'. *Journal of Interdisciplinary Gender Studies: JIGS*, 4(2): 81–98.

'Wollongong'. *World Population Review*. https://worldpopulation review.com/cities/australia/wollongong (accessed 27 August 2024).

Zuel, B. (2007), 'Young Modern'. *The Sydney Morning Herald*, 31 March. https://www.smh.com.au/entertainment/young -modern-20070331-gdpt2l.html (accessed 23 June 2024).

Discography

Silverchair (1994), *Tomorrow*. Murmur.

Silverchair (1995), *Frogstomp*. Murmur.

Silverchair (1997), *Freak Show*. Murmur.

Silverchair (1999), *Neon Ballroom*. Murmur.

Silverchair (2002), *Diorama*. Eleven.

Silverchair (2007), *Young Modern*. Eleven.

Podcasts and recordings

Eastley, T., and Turtle, M. (2007), 'Silverchair Set Award Record at ARIAs Program'. *ABC Listen*, 29 October. https://www.abc.net.au/listen/programs/am/silverchair-set-award-record-at-arias/2600164 (accessed 25 June 2024).

Grynberg, S. (2023), 'Ben Gillies on the Text Message that Ended Silverchair'. *Stories of Us*, 15 November. https://podcasts.apple.com/au/podcast/ben-gillies-on-the-text-message-that-ended-silverchair/id1710999188?i=1000634810361 (accessed 14 July 2024).

Hedger, D. (2020), 'Episode 2: Frogstomp'. *Too Much of Not Enough: A Silverchair Podcast*, 16 May. Apple. (accessed 1 April 2024).

Hedger, D. (2021), 'Episode 17: Conversation with John Watson'. *Too Much of Not Enough: A Silverchair Podcast*, 5 June. Apple. (accessed 2 April 2024).

Johns, D. (2021), 'Episodes 1, 2 and 3'. *Who is Daniel Johns?* Spotify. (accessed 2 April 2024).

triple j. (2015a), '1975-1985: 40 Years of triple j'. *The J Files*. Available online: https://www.abc.net.au/listen/programs/the-j-files/1975-1985-40-years-of-triple-j/10274876 (accessed 9 March 2024).

triple j. (2015b), '1985-1995: 40 Years of triple j'. *The J Files*. Available online: https://www.abc.net.au/listen/programs/the-j-files/1985 -1995-40-years-of-triple-j/10274872 (accessed 9 March 2024).

Videos

ARIA. (1995), '1995 ARIA Awards – Performances and Moments'. Available online: https://www.youtube.com/playlist?list=PLy jeYZ2qUJzxTcFCgsEjZytTsREytwS3Q (accessed 27 March 2024).

Australian Story. (2023), 'A Silver Lining, Part Two'. Producer: Ben Cheshire. Australian Broadcasting Commission.

Great Australian Albums. 'Diorama by Silverchair'. (2007), Producers: Larry Meltzer and Toby Creswell. Special Broadcasting Service.

Laj, M. (1995), 'Silverchair 09-17-1995 Santa Monica Pier, Santa Monica, CA (including MTV News clip)'. Available online: https://www.youtube.com/watch?v=_6cJsYE_wGI (accessed 27 March 2024).

Live2CD. (undated), 'Silverchair - Straight Lines (Jay Leno, July 10th, 2007)'. *YouTube*. https://www.youtube.com/watch?v =fOU9LMME9fg (accessed 8 June 2024).

Much Music. (1995), 'Interview with Daniel [Johns] on MuchMusic 1995'. Available online: https://www.youtube.com/watch?v =64EsR8Gd2pw (accessed 26 March 2024).

Pure Massacre (1995), [Australian music video]. Dir. Robert Hambling. Available online: https://www.youtube.com/watch ?v=2oPBBRpaJFI (accessed 1 February 2024).

Pure Massacre (1996), [US music video]. Dir. Peter Christopherson. Available online: https://www.youtube.com/watch?v =c6wMH2AGbwg (accessed 1 February 2024).

Index